the
ALPINE PASS
ROUTE

A Walking Guide Across The Swiss Alps.

by
Jonathan Hurdle

(To my parents)

Dark Peak Publishers
(Sheffield, England)

This edition: 1983
Dark Peak Ltd
336 Abbey Lane,
Sheffield, England

ISBN 0 9506272 9 1

© Jonathan Hurdle.

Maps drawn by Angela Williams with additional
artwork by Paul Surrey.

Printed by Heanor Gate Printing Ltd
Heanor, Derbyshire.

Contents

INTRODUCTION   7

EQUIPMENT   9

FITNESS 10

MAP NOTES 10

COMPASS 11

EMERGENCY EQUIPMENT AND SAFETY 11

ACCOMMODATION 12

THE COUNTRY CODE 13

LANGUAGE 13

WALKING SPEED 14

ROUTE-FINDING 14

DRINKING 15

BIRDS IN THE ALPS 15

ALPINE FLOWERS 16

ALPINE VERNACULAR 16

SPECIALIST EQUIPMENT 16

SEASON 17

GETTING THERE 17

Continued overleaf . .

Contents continued . . .

DAY 1 — Sargans — Weisstannen 19

DAY 2 — Weisstannen — Foopass — Elm 21

DAY 3 — Elm — Richetlipass — Linthal 25

DAY 4 — Linthal — Urner Boden Valley —
Klausenpass — Unterschächen — Altdorf . . 31

DAY 5 — Altdorf — Surenenpass — Engelberg 37

DAY 6 — Engelberg — Jochpass — Meiringen 41

DAY 7 — Meiringen — Grosse Scheidegg —
Grindelwald 45

DAY 8 — Grindelwald — Kleine Scheidegg —
Lauterbrunnen 49

DAY 9 — Lauterbrunnen — Mürren —
Sefinenfurke — Griesalp 53

DAY 10 — Griesalp — Hohtürli — Kandersteg 57

DAY 11 — Kandersteg — Bunderchrinde —
Adelboden 61

DAY 12 — Adelboden — Hahnenmoospass —
Lenk 65

DAY 13 — Lenk — Truttlisbergpass — Gstaad 69

DAY 14 — Gstaad — Col de Jable —
L'Etivaz/La Lecherette 73

DAY 15 — L'Etivaz/La Lecherette —
Col de Jaman — Montreux 79

KEY TO MAPS

Road

Track/path

River/stream

Village/town

Railway with station

Cable car

Cliffs

Marsh

Camp site

Mountain peak

Church

Views

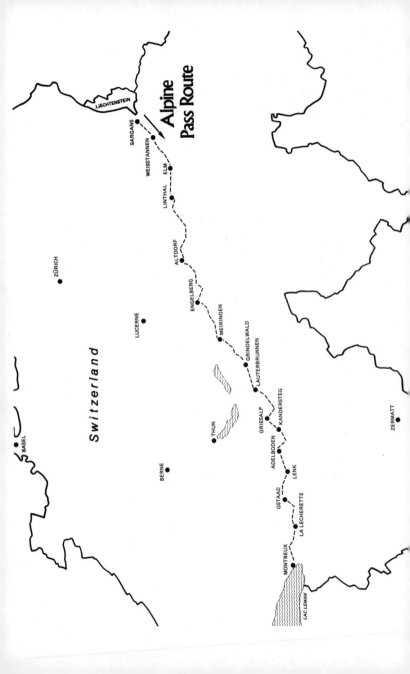

Introduction

Introduction

The Alpine Pass Route is a little-known long-distance footpath which runs along the northern side of the Swiss Alps from the north-east to the south-west of the country.

On its 200-mile journey from Sargans, near the Liechtenstein border, to Montreux, on Lake Geneva, the route takes in the entire range of breathtaking Alpine scenery — from the lush meadows of the Bernese Oberland to the forbidding North Face of the Eiger; from the famous Jungfrau to the remote valleys at its western end.

In between its more famous landmarks, it passes through the sleepy valley towns of Linthal and Lenk, visits the glamorous tourist magnets of Grindelwald and Gstaad, and winds over the passes of Kleine Scheidegg and the Hohturli.

As its name suggests, the main features of the Alpine Pass Route are the passes between the mountains. The route has 14 of these traditional routes of access between valleys, the highest being some 2,800m and most at well over 2,000m. Far below lie the valleys which the APR also passes through, so making a walking tour with great variations in height and constantly steep gradients.

This guide is an attempt — believed to be the first in English — to open up a high level and yet accessible route through some of Europe's most beautiful high country.

The beauty — in both senses — of the APR is that it offers the walker a constant array of magnificent scenery without him or her having to retreat to remote and inaccessible areas. The wildness of some of the terrain is complemented by its proximity to towns, so that it is possible to be safely tucked up in a Swiss hotel at the end of every day's walking.

Despite the severity of the APR by the standards of British walking, it should be within the capabilities of anyone with some walking experience who is reasonably fit and has at least two weeks to spare. The APR is not a mountaineering expedition, despite its altitude. Its higher sections are likely to have some snow, even in summer, but these demand equipment no more specialised than a pair of crampons and an ice axe. From late June to mid-September, no technical mountaineering knowledge is needed and only the normal mountain safety precautions need be taken.

As befits its Swiss-ness, the paths which make up the route are admirably well-marked, so that route-finding is mostly elementary and the ability to navigate by map and compass, whilst a necessary skill, is not often likely to be needed.

The APR was born, so far as the author can ascertain, in the Swiss National Tourist Office booklet 'On foot through Switzerland', now out of print. The route never achieved official recognition and does not now officially exist. It was the name given to an amalgamation of pre-existing footpaths, all of which are administered by the different cantons they run through, but none of which come under the auspices of any kind of central authority. The APR was therefore purely a product of the imagination of someone in the tourist office who then drew a line on a map and published some very cursory details in the aforementioned booklet. For this reason, the walker will not find a single sign saying 'Alpine Pass Route.' There is apparently no prospect of the route becoming officially recognised because of the federal system of Swiss government. But perhaps this book will change all that.

For walkers who have risen to the challenges of the Pennine Way or the Lake District and want something of a slightly higher order, or for those simply wishing to explore the Alps in the best possible way, the Alpine Pass Route is both a strenuous expedition and a visual extravaganza. It is a memorable experience within reach of anyone who cares to take the trouble.

Equipment

Most people will already be familiar with basic walking equipment. Equipment need not be highly specialised but should not be skimped on. A strong pair of boots is the most basic essential and should be well worn-in before starting out. Much of the route is over rough stony track and nothing short of good boots will protect the soles of your feet and your ankles from the punishment these surfaces can inflict. The waterproof leather upper of all good walking boots is equally essential for keeping out the icy water and snow which you are bound to walk through from time to time. A wide range of boots is stocked in sports and specialist walking shops and you should look for: one-piece leather uppers; a Vibram sole at least half-an-inch thick (some people prefer rigid-soled boots); a stiff back of the boot to support the heel; scree cuffs to keep stones out and protect the ankles; room inside for two pairs of socks, bearing in mind that feet expand when walking under a load. There is a current trend towards lightweight walking boots and you would be well advised to discuss your requirements with a specialist retailer. Nylon or canvas gaiters to fasten to the top of the boot will protect the lower leg from mud, stones, water or snow.

A complete layer of outer clothing is essential and this should be water- and wind-proof. Even in high summer, the wind in the mountains can be very cold, so you should have an outer layer — anorak and overtrousers — which allows you to walk without generating too much condensation inside the garments. Thin nylon anoraks generate condensation as well as tending to let water in from the outside, and so should be avoided. Substantial nylon garments keep you mostly dry and are light to carry, so are probably the best bet. You should take a hat and gloves.

Your rucksack needs to be chosen carefully and, as your feet should be thoroughly familiar with your boots before you start out, so your back and shoulders should be well-acquainted with a rucksack. Its capacity clearly depends on how much you want to carry in it and this in turn depends on whether you intend to provide your own accommodation (ie. a tent) and catering. On warm-up walks, you will find out whether any part of the rucksack is uncomfortable to your shoulders, back or hips. Pack it carefully, taking care not to put any hard items where they will stick into your back. Remember, no rucksack is totally waterproof, so it pays to use a strong plastic bin liner as an inner skin to keep your things dry. Be absolutely ruthless in packing it and dispose of any item which is not completely necessary. You will regret every unnecessary ounce on the way up the first pass.

Take lightweight versions of everything if you can, and remember that dried food is quite palatable if cooked properly. But be careful about economising on weight. While you may be able to get away without taking a plate on the assumption that (assuming you are doing your own catering) you will eat out of your mug, you could be in trouble by throwing out an extra pullover or spare pair of socks.

Fitness

If you are stiff and sore about a few hours' walking on the South Downs, do not attempt the APR until you are fitter. Climbing 3,000ft with no break in the gradient whilst carrying 35lbs on your back, is a task not to be taken lightly and you should be confident you are able to do it before setting out. Remember that 3,000ft is almost as high as the highest mountains in England. If you are fairly used to vigorous exercise, a few practice walks simulating the conditions of the real thing as far as possible should be sufficient. If you do not take any form of regular exercise, the problem is more serious and you will need to work at getting fit over a good few weeks if you are to enjoy the walk to the full.

Maps

Despite the well-trodden and well-signposted nature of many of the APR's paths, good maps are essential. The ones to get are the Swiss equivalent of the Ordnance Survey, known in German as the *Landeskarte der Schweiz* and in French as *Carte Nationale de la Suisse*. They are excellent and provide the walker with all the navigational information he or she needs. Curiously, though, they are published without an attached legend. This is contained in a separate booklet which explains all the symbols, although these are mostly self-evident. The sheets you need are: 237 Walenstadt; 245 Stans; 246 Klausenpass; 247 Sardona; 254 Interlaken; 255 Sustenpass; 262 Rochers de Naye; 263 Wildstrubel and 264 Jungfrau. Most numbers are kept in stock by Westcol Productions Ltd, Goring, Reading, Berks. They can also be ordered through the Swiss National Tourist Office, 1 New Coventry Street, London W1V 3HG (Tel. 01 734 1921), but this may take some time as they are not kept in stock and have to be ordered from Switzerland.

Maps, when being used, should be kept in a clear plastic map holder, fastened with Velcro. This is a vital piece of equipment as it protects the map which would otherwise quickly become badly damaged and probably illegible.

Compass

An ordinary Silva compass and an ability to navigate by it are essential. Preferably there should be one compass for each member of the group in case he/she gets separated from the rest.

Emergency Equipment and Safety

Despite the nearness of towns to much of the route, safety precautions must be taken seriously. Carry a first aid kit containing all the usual medications, especially dressings and antiseptic creams for blisters, ointment for insect bites and plenty of sun tan cream.

Carry a stock of emergency rations in case you have to spend an unexpected night in the mountains. Take plenty of high energy foods in your emergency kit, but also for eating along the route. It is possible that you will find your energy level severely depleted from time to time and this can be remedied by eating chocolate, dried fruit, glucose tablets and so on. Fast energy sources like this can be invaluable towards the end of a day's walking.

If you become lost or stranded on a mountainside in darkness or cloud, keeping warm is top priority. A large plastic bag (which you get inside) or a foil blanket are vital for helping to stop loss of body heat.

A torch and/or a whistle can be useful for letting a search party know where you are. The standard distress signal is six blasts on a whistle, six shouts or six repetitions of anything, followed by a minute's silence and then repeated.

Route planning for a day's walking is vital. Be careful about estimating the distance you want to go and the time it will take you. Do not attempt to cross a pass if there is a chance there will not be sufficient daylight for you to get down the other side and find a campsite or accommodation for the night.

The recommended minimum number for any walking trip is three people and this is especially true with the APR. If one of the party gets injured, one can stay with the injured person while the other goes for help. A larger party of perhaps six is recommended, so that each person will have a better chance of finding someone whose pace matches their own. Theoretically, a party should always go at the pace of its slowest member, but inevitably the group will get strung out as people travel at different speeds.

Accommodation

After a hard day in the mountains it is possible at the end of every day to collapse into a hot bath and a clean bed in one of Switzerland's renowned hotels. Every town on the route has plenty of them, and details of some of the cheaper ones are given here. Further information on them can be obtained from the Swiss National Tourist Office in London.

For those wanting simpler accommodation, there are six Youth Hostels en route, and advance booking is strongly recommended for these, especially in summer.

For walkers on a shoe-string budget or those who simply relish the thought of camping in the Alps and are prepared to carry the extra weight, there are plenty of official campsites at the major tourist centres such as Engelberg, Grindelwald and Kandersteg, but they are thin on the ground at either end of the route. Campsite fees range between one and seven Swiss Francs per person per night, and tend to go up during the high season of July and August. Many campsites recognise valid AIT/FICC/FIA camping cards and booklets.

But if you really want to get away from it all, unofficial campsites are by far the best and these, of course, are unlimited. Outside the towns there are any number of idyllic spots where you can pitch a tent for the night undisturbed and with an endless supply of clear, cold mountain water flowing by. Remember that most of these 'unofficial' sites will be on farmland and you should do the farmer the courtesy of asking if he minds you camping on his land — if, of course, he is anywhere to be seen.

The Country Code

This simple code of rules, well-known by users of the British countryside, applies just as much in the Alps as on the South Downs. The freedom to camp and walk in the wilds will only exist so long as it is not abused. Remember, therefore, to:

Guard against all risk of fire.
Fasten all gates.
Keep dogs under control.
Keep to rights of way across farmland.
Avoid damaging fences, hedges and walls.
Leave no litter.
Safeguard water supplies.
Protect wildlife, plants and trees.
Go carefully on country roads.

Language

German is spoken throughout most of Switzerland and this applies also to the Alpine Pass Route. An elementary knowledge will get you by for most of it. Even if you have no German, this should not present too many difficulties as the Swiss are notoriously good linguists, especially when it

comes to looking after tourists. As you cross the penultimate pass, some 25 miles from the end of the APR, you
go abruptly into French-speaking Switzerland. If you have
no French either, don't worry because you are only a
stone's throw from multilingual Montreux.

Walking Speed

The times given at the beginning of each day's guide can
only be a rough approximation. They are based on personal
experience, assuming an overall average speed for a day's
walking, which includes climbing a pass, would be about
two-miles-an-hour. You should take into account all the
factors peculiar to your own expedition when deciding how
long a certain section is going to take you. The official
advice is that you should allow an extra hour over your flat
rate of travel for every 457m (1,500ft) to be climbed.

Route-finding

Most of the paths on the Alpine Pass Route are well-marked
with signs giving the direction in which you have to travel,
the principal destinations of a footpath and the estimated
time it will take you to get there. These times (mostly
marked in 'Std.' meaning *stunden*, the German for 'hours'),
somehow cater for the 'average walker' and so are a fairly
reliable guide to go by.

There are two main types of signs the APR walker will
come across. The most common is the 'Bergweg' or mountain path sign which, in addition to a bright yellow plate
bearing the name of a town and, at certain intervals, the
time it will take you to get there, may have a red stripe on a
white background forming an arrow at the end of the sign.
This red on white also appears on small signs on its own and
is frequently painted on rocks, trees, fence-posts, mountain
huts or anywhere else it can be of use to the walker. These
red and white markers are quite conspicuous in the mountains and are extremely useful throughout the APR, especially where the footpath is indistinct.

The other type of sign on the APR, and far less
common, differs from the Bergweg signs in that it has no
red markings. These signs denote a 'Central Lowlands
Footpath'.

Drinking

Replacing lost body fluid becomes a major issue on the Alpine Pass Route, especially when climbing a pass on a hot day. Natural water is plentifully available for most of the route and its usual sources are streams, which frequently cross your path, and the water troughs often found outside farms and other buildings. In the experience of our party, these were always pure and we drank from both sources unrestrictedly. To be quite safe, though, purification tablets can do no harm.

Despite the abundance of water pouring down the mountains, it is also necessary to carry — and frequently fill up — a water bottle, especially for the high stretches. For beverages of a more interesting nature, see Chapter Nine. Just to prove that you have not let yourself in for a totally ascetic experience, I will turn from Drinking to:

Birds in the Alps

For bird-watching walkers, there are a number of species to look out for which you should be able to add to your ticklists without much fear of being upstaged by fellow twitchers who confine themselves to British shores.

The cognoscenti will excuse the elementary notes on some of the birds you are likely to see along the APR. Perhaps the most spectacular is the Black Woodpecker. This crow-size bird, far larger than any British woodpecker, is all black except for a flaming red crown. You may find it in mature coniferous and beech woods. Another central European species, occurring only accidentally in the British Isles, is the Wall Creeper. With ash-grey back, and white spotted crimson wings, it certainly upstages its dowdy British relative the Tree Creeper. It also lives up to its name as it can be seen creeping up walls with fluttering, hesitant shuffles.

A more usual sight is the Alpine Chough which can often be seen high in the mountains. It differs from the Chough mainly in its much shorter and straighter yellow bill. Another Alpine variety of a familiar British summer visitor is the Alpine Swift. This is much larger and browner than the Swift with white underparts and a brown breast band. A relative of the dull old British Dunnock is the Alpine Accentor, which may be seen at high altitudes, as may Snow Buntings. Birds of prey include Golden Eagles which can often be seen circling high in the mountains, and Black Kites which you may be able to see hunting above Lake Leman.

Alpine Flowers

The Alps are famous for their wild flowers which exist under extreme conditions of temperature and terrain. Some of the better-known species are: Gentian, Alpine Pansy, Primula, Globe Flower, Silver Thistle, Soldanella, Martagon Lily, Alpine Edelweiss, Alpine Poppy, Glacier Buttercup and a variety of Saxifrages.

Alpine Vernacular

Not a kind of railway but a type of language, brought into common usage by mountaineers and likely to be also of interest to those who prefer more modest mountain pursuits. An *aiguille* is a needle-sharp peak; an *arete* is a sharp ridge and *brunnen* is the term for fountains or springs. A *cabane* is a refuge hut, while a *col* is the culminating point of a pass. *Crap* diverges from its English usage in being the Romansch for rock, and *furka* comes from the German, meaning pass. *Joch* is also German for a yoke or a pass. A *matte* is a pasture. *Sass* is the ancient local word for stone or rock while narrow, steep paths are known as *steigs*.

Specialist Equipment

The most specialised mountain equipment you could conceivably need is a pair of crampons, an ice axe and some rope. These are included as optional extras in the equipment list, for they are not likely to be strictly necessary. There may be snow on some of the passes, especially if you are walking at either end of the season, and a pair of crampons could make climbing snow-covered final approaches a lot easier.

It is also worth bearing in mind that at the beginning of

the season (until mid-July) the snow will be melting and there could be a danger of falling through it in some places. Ropes to keep your party together could, therefore, add to the safety of your expedition. But the occasions you are likely to need these items of equipment will be few and far between and you will need to think whether you are prepared to carry the extra weight.

Season

This is dependent on the snow, which starts to melt properly in June and should be gone by the end of July. Late June until early October is the recommended period for walking the Alpine Pass Route.

Getting There

Switzerland's rail network is superb and connects with main lines from all over Europe. The most direct way to get to Sargans from England is via Basel. You can get a direct train there from one of the continental channel ports. You will have to change there for a train to Sargans.

Montreux is situated on one of the main lines from Italy and you can get fast through trains to Paris from there.

DAY 1 Sargans - Weisstannen

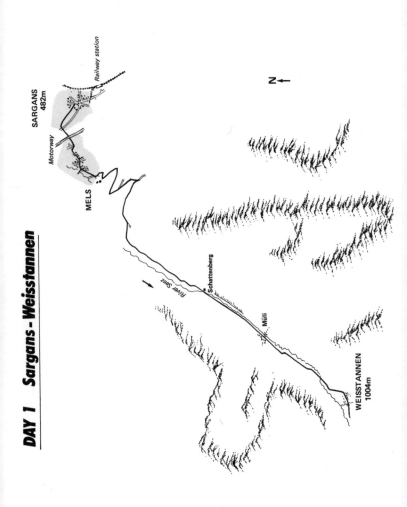

Day 1

Sargans — Weisstannen
14km/8¾ miles (4 hours)

Terrain: *Easy roads.*
Altitude: *Sargans (482m). Weisstannen (1004m).*
Maps: *Sheet 237 Walenstadt.*
Views: *The Rhein Valley as you climb up towards the Weisstannental. Mountains to the west as you approach Weisstanen.*

If you need easing into the Alpine Pass Route, this is the perfect way to do it. No more than half a day's walk and a gradual tarmacced climb to the pretty village of Weisstannen at the head of the valley of the same name. From the centre of Sargans, follow roads in a north-westerly direction and aim to go under the motorway running in between Sargans and Mels. Head for Mels, looking out for signs to Weisstannen. Walk through Mels and, as you start to climb, look out for the Mels Youth Hostel on your right.

After Mels, it is a long steady climb up a zig-zag road until it starts to level out, after which it is almost a straight run to Weisstannen. The view behind you of the Rhein Valley steadily gets more extensive until you get into the pine forest above the River Seez.

Mels offers your first taste of chocolate-box Swiss architecture. On your way up the hill you will see little wooden chalets with ornate woodworking on the balcony and the eves, and nearly always adorned with brilliant displays of geraniums in window boxes.

You will pass Postbus stops every couple of miles. Despite being apparently in the middle of nowhere, they have seats as well as timetables printed in three languages — German, French and Italian.

If the wooden chalets in Mels came straight off the cover of a chocolate box, Weisstannen is the perfect setting for such a scene. It is a small village nestling beneath peaks which may well be snow-covered and on whose sides cattle graze contentedly with their constantly clanging bells. It has an hotel and an immaculately-kept village church worth a respectful look. You should find a map of the area fixed to a wall on your right as you head west out of the village. This map shows the various walking routes in the area and these are colour-marked according to the degree of severity.

Just beyond the map are some yellow direction signs, one of which (to Foopass and Elm) you will follow tomorrow if you are staying in Weisstannen overnight.

Camping: There are plenty of places to camp if you follow the Foopass signs upstream for two or three kilometres. But beware of cows!

Accommodation: Weisstannen has two hotels, the Alpenhof (Tel. 085 217 63) and the Gemse (Tel. 085 217 05).

Day 2

Weisstannen — Foopass — Elm
22km/13¾ miles (7 hours)

Terrain: *Mostly rough but firm track. A steep climb from Untersass to the upper Seez Valley. Long gradual descent into Elm.*
Altitude: *Weisstannen (1004m). Foopass (2223m). Elm (977m).*
Maps: *Sheet 247 Sardona.*
Views: *Chli Schiben Gros and Surenstock from the hut below the Foopass. The view from the Foopass in both directions.*

This is the first real climb of the APR. At the western end of Weisstannen village follow the yellow waymarking sign towards Foopass and Elm. This takes you over the bridge across the River Seez and up the road which by now has become smaller and less well-made. It runs parallel to the river for five kilometres or so. As a break from the road, you can take a track which leads off into the woods about two kilometres west of Weisstannen. It rejoins the road at the farm settlement of Vørsiez. You should continue along the road, keeping to the south side of the river until the end of the valley.

The gigantic bulk of Foostock, Surenstock and Chli Schiben Gros now towers around you, apparently blocking an exit from the valley and heralding a hard climb.

Follow the road to the farm at Glätti, shortly after which it crosses the river to the north side and continues towards Untersäss. As the road peters out above Untersäss you will see a yellow sign a short way above you to the right. Ignore that sign and look instead for a red and white

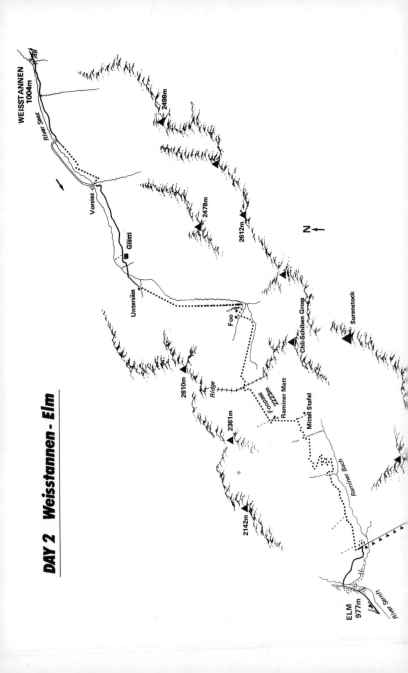

DAY 2 Weisstannen - Elm

WEISSTANNEN
1004m

River Seez

Vorsiez

Glätti

Untersäss

Foo

2498m

2478m

2612m

N

Surenstock

Chli-Schiben Gross

2610m

Ridge

Foopass
2223m

Raminer Matt

Mittel Stafel

2361m

Raminer Bach

2142m

ELM
977m

River Sernft

waymarker painted on a rock about half-way across a field to your right. This leads to the beginning of a steep zig-zag path which will lead you to an upper valley where the River Seez originates. In looking for the beginning of the zig-zag, you need to stick fairly close to the river all the way up the valley, so do not stray too far from it.

After about two kilometres, the track stops crossing the contours and runs comfortingly with them along the western bank of the Seez. You may have to cross patches of snow across this path, so beware if they are melting. There are likely to be much larger patches of snow on the mountains above you and these are worth watching to catch sight of the famous mountain antelope, the chamois and the mountain rodent, the marmot.

The chamois is known as a goat-like antelope because of its similarity to both animals. It stands about two-and-a-half-feet high and has a thick chestnut brown coat and short horns. It is famous for its agility in the mountains. It spends much of the year in herds of 15 to 20, living in woods on mountains and feeding on grass and lichens. During the summer, some animals leave the herd and live for some weeks in the snow fields and glaciers above the forests. It is here that it is most likely to be seen by Alpine walkers.

The marmot is more often heard than seen and its distinctive squeak will become familiar on the APR. It is a small, stout rodent related to the squirrel, is up to two-feet-long and is covered in coarse, reddish brown hair. It lives in large colonies and can often be seen scampering across the snow.

After about two kilometres walking along the bank of the River Seez, the path turns abruptly up to the right to make a short but very steep climb to three buildings marked on the map simply as 'Foo'. It is a fine place for a rest before making the final approach to the pass, as there is a wonderful view across the end of the Seez Valley to Chli Schiben Gros, Alplichopf and other mountains.

From the top of the steep track, head towards the main building. Behind it is a yellow sign giving walking times to various places, including the Foopass and Elm.

Over the Elm sign it says 'Nach dem Bach rechts'. This means you have to cross the stream by the hut and then turn right. Do not be tempted to go up the nearest west-facing valley, despite the fact that it is going roughly in the direction of the Foopass.

After crossing the stream, head briefly in a south-westerly direction and walk around the edge of a ridge running east-west and almost leading up to the pass itself. You should soon pick up red and white markers which are painted on rocks and wooden posts at regular intervals most of the way to the pass. The final approach is a steady climb across ground which may be very wet if the snow is melting. This last kilometre or so is not steep and should leave you in a reasonable state to enjoy the view from the top. One down, 13 to go.

Leave the pass by the track, but watch the dog-leg in it a few hundred yards down. Turn sharp left there and then keep an eye out for red and white markers on rocks on the way down the mountain towards the farm buildings at Raminer Matt. Walk through the farm and then begin the more gradual descent down a winding woodland track into Elm. It is a picturesque farm track, passing through woods and meadows, past little farm chalets and with frequent glimpses into the valley containing the Raminer Bach far below.

At Elm you will be able to replenish stores and rest after the first real day's walking. It is a sleepy sort of town, but the chances are you will be too.

Camping: There is no official campsite in Elm, but it is possible to put a tent up next to the noisy Raminer Bach, about half-a-kilometre above the town, upstream from a number of picnic sites. The wooded area in question can be reached from the path you have come down or via a footpath from the town centre which runs up the side of the bach.

Accommodation: Elm has a two-star hotel, the Elmer (Tel. 058 86 17 66).

Above: *The Weisstannen Valley; on route to the Foopass.*
Below: *Descending the Richetli Pass on Day 3. A typical alpine hut. (Photos: Jill Ranford).*

Above: *At the entrance to the Urner Boden valley, Day 4.*
Below: *Looking back down the Urner Boden from the top of Klausenpass. (Photos: Jill Ranford).*

Above: *The village of Ásch, looking back towards Klausenpass. (Photo: Jill Ranford).* **Below:** *The town of Meiringen reached at the end of Day 6; noted for its church with 11th and 12th century frescos. (Photo: Swiss National Tourist Office).*

Above: *Grindelwald, reached at the end of Day 7. In the left background, the Wetterhorn. (Photo: Swiss National Tourist Office).*

Above: *Lauterbrunnen, end of Day 8 destination. (Photo: Swiss National Tourist Office).*

Above: *The village of Kandersteg. The Alpine Pass Route app-roaches up the valley beyond and leaves to the left from this view. Above the village stands the Balmhorn (3712m). (Photo: Swiss National Tourist Office).*

Above: *Looking back to Kandersteg from Hohtürli on Day 10. (Photo: Nick Turner).*
Below: *Adelboden, Day 11, a typical village of the Bernese Oberland. (Photo: Swiss National Tourist Office).*

Above: *Montreux, the journey's end. In view the famous Chillon Castle by Lake Geneva. (Photo: Swiss National Tourist Office).*

Day 3

Elm — Richetlipass — Linthal
20km/12½ miles (7 hours)

Terrain: *Hard climb to the Richetlipass — early stages steep and rocky. Final approach to the pass may have snow. Steep descent initially.*
Altitude: *Elm (977m). Richetlipass (2261m). Linthal (653m).*
Maps: *Sheet 247 Sardona, Sheet 246 Klausenpass.*
Views: *The Richetlipass from the hut on its eastern side. Both eastwards and westwards from the pass.*

Follow the main road south-west out of Elm and begin a gradual climb. After about two kilometres the road becomes unmade, but still in quite good condition as it evidently carries military traffic from the installation at the top of the valley. You have to walk right past this installation and you may find your way barred near the point where the road forks to Walenbrugg. A sentry may be posted here to stop people and traffic going near whatever kind of military activity goes on there. But this is apparently only for short periods, so do not be tempted to take another route to the Richetlipass.

　　Turn right off the road at the Walenbrugg buildings and walk up the north side of the river for about one kilometre. Cross the river over a concrete bridge and shortly afterwards cross a small tributary of it. You are now on the south side of the river and you should follow the track up, picking your way over an increasing quantity of boulders and scree. The track effectively peters out on this side of the river and you must cross another tributary of it to find the path up towards the pass. The bottom of this path has a grid reference of approximately 726.3E 196.7N. It climbs

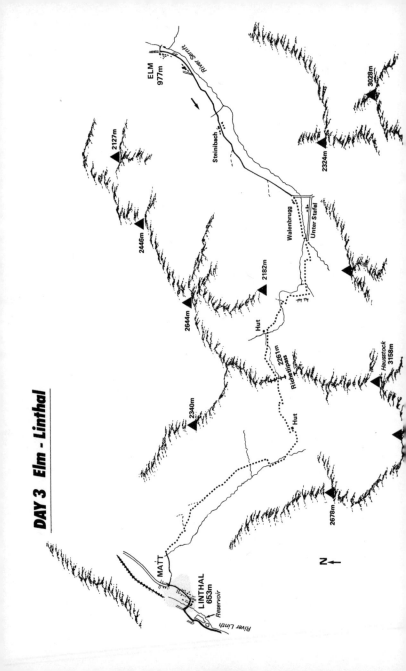

DAY 3 Elm - Linthal

ELM
977m

River Sernft

2127m

Steinibach

3028m

2324m

2446m

Walenbrugg

Unter Stafel

2644m

2182m

Hut

2340m

2261m
Richetlipass

Hut

Hausstock
3158m

2678m

MATT

LINTHAL
653m

River Linth

Reservoir

N

steeply up the mountain in a northerly direction. This is a tough, winding climb.

As you near the top, the ground becomes less steep and the path heads towards the river which soon tumbles down into the valley you have just climbed out of. Take care not to take the path which crosses the river lower than you want and winds round the side of the Erbser Stock. There is no bridge across these upper reaches and you may need to go some way upstream to find a crossing point. Alternatively, you may be able to cross a snow 'bridge' which could have formed in the river's gully. If so, be extremely careful about this and try to ascertain whether the snow will hold your weight before crossing. Remember, the river is flowing fast and furious underneath.

Once back on the north side of the river, you will need to scramble up a steep bank and then continue upstream, crossing a small brook and eventually coming to a mountain hut at the head of the upper valley and directly below the Richetlipass.

If the hut is open, it may be worth taking a breather there before the final climb to the pass. From here you will get your first proper view of the pass and it is a daunting sight, especially if covered in snow. The Richetlipass is probably the wildest, most isolated pass on the APR and climbing it is one of the high points of the trip.

From the hut (GR: 725.5E 195.6N) follow the line of the bach straight up the middle of the valley. This may not be possible if there is snow and you will have to pick your way towards the top of the pass along the sides of the valley and up the steep final approach. Be very careful if you are walking across snow in the summer months. Remember it is melting from underneath as well as from on top. Crampons and ice axes could come in handy on this section and members of the party could be roped together for extra safety.

The pass itself is just a razor edge of soil and rock, but you get a real 'roof of the world' feeling when you get there as you survey the valley you have just climbed up and distant peaks to the east and west. It should take at least half-an-hour to climb there from the hut.

From the top (and you are by now on sheet 246 Klaus-enpass) head for another hut (GR: 722.8E 195.1N) situated on a spur of the mountainside above the River Durnagel which flows down into Linthal. The path down to the hut is steep and winding, but you are helped by the red and white markers. If you are running out of daylight or energy you can probably stay the night at the hut, which is very basic but at least provides a roof over your head. It contains a straw 'bed' in one corner which is *not* recommended. There is also a primitive stove, a rough table and some benches.

If you are continuing to Linthal (about two-hours' walk from the hut) you need to keep your wits about you to find the path after leaving the hut. Head towards the end of the spur and look for a red and white marker. From there the path slopes steeply away to the left below a small cliff and over some scree. After this it is fairly well-trodden and gradually levels out as you get down to the river.

At the river, cross a new bridge (which can be seen from the hut) and follow a field downstream for about half-a-kilometre. Cross back again before you get to some farm buildings, by a mini-hydroelectric scheme. From here you have a pleasant walk through woods and fields down into Linthal.

Linthal is a rather austere little town, despite the beauty of the valley it sits in. But it has one or two cafes for beers and schnitzels, and shops to replenish your stores. The standard of Swiss hospitality is famous and even the cheaper eating houses are no exception. The food is invariably delicious — hot, perfectly cooked and charmingly served. Of course, you pay for it, but after a day or two in the mountains you probably won't begrudge a few francs for a decent meal.

Camping: There is no official site in Linthal and it is not easy to find an unofficial one. In order to, you must walk out of town on the Klausenpass road and turn left off it by the first of its zig-zags up the mountain. Follow a small road past a hydroelectric station, keeping parallel to the river which flows through the centre of the town. Continue walking south until you get into the woods where, on your right, you should find a number of places suitable for pitching a tent.

Accommodation: Linthal has a two-star hotel, the Hotel Bahnhof (Tel. 58 84 15 22).

DAY 4 (part 1) Linthal–Altdorf

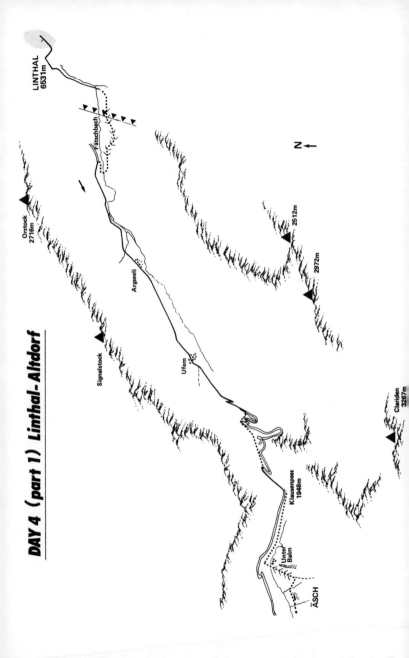

LINTHAL 6531m

Orstock 2716m

Signalstock

Fätschbach

Argseeli

Ufem

Klausenpass 1948m

Unter Balm

ÄSCH

Clariden 3287m

2512m

2972m

N

Day 4

**Linthal — Urner Boden Valley — Klausenpass
— Unterschächen — Altdorf**
32km/20 miles (9 hours)

Terrain: *Steepish climb from Linthal valley up to the Klausenpass road. Then gradual gradients most of the way to the pass. Steep descent from the pass. A lot of road walking.*
Altitude: *Linthal (653m). Klausenpass (1948m). Unterschächen (995m). Altdorf (458m).*
Maps: *Sheet 246 Klausenpass.*
Views: *The Urner Boden Valley. Asch below the Klausenpass.*

The length of today's walk is necessary if Engelberg is to be reached the next day from Altdorf. Walkers who are camping will clearly have more flexibility but for those without a tent, town-hopping is a vital part of this itinerary. Day four is a long walk, but not too strenuous in terms of gradients to be climbed. If you feel you can cope with extra distance tomorrow, Unterschächen and Spiringen are good places to stop for the night. But remember there is no accommodation between Altdorf and Engelberg.

Day four involves by far the largest amount of road walking of any day in this itinerary. But it has its compensations, the main one being the Urner Boden valley, billed by the tourist literature as one of the most beautiful Alpine valleys in Switzerland — and with no exaggeration. Despite the traffic, the road is certainly the best place from which to view this extraordinary place.

From the centre of Linthal, take the road past the hydroelectric station, as instructed for last night's camping. Follow this road parallel to the river for about one

DAY 4 (part 2) Linthal - Altdorf

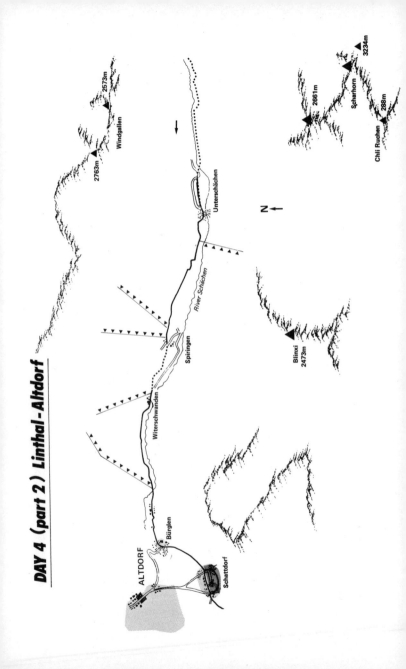

kilometre. Shortly after it crosses the Fatschbach, follow the sign to the Klausenpass up a small track going up into the woods on your right. This is a steep muddy zig-zag path through lovely beech woods and meadows towards the main road leading to the pass. The path levels out as you near the Urner Boden valley and you cross back across the Fatschbach shortly before joining the road.

You will be guided all the way up by red and white markers and these peter out when you get to the road. The gradient soon becomes easier and the valley gradually unfolds before you. It is one of the high points of the APR, as you walk along the floor of the wide valley with the craggy Jegerstock towering above you to the north and a more gradual slope up to the Gemsfairenstock to the south. The lush green of the valley floor stretches as far up the mountains as the gradient will allow and the air is filled with the constant clank of cowbells. The cattle are a famous feature of this valley — because there are so many of them — and they wander apparently unchecked, frequently forcing motorists to stop and let them pass.

The Klausenpass is quite a distant prospect and you may want to stop for a rest or a drink at Ufem. As you climb out of the valley at the western end, red and white markers will guide you up a path which cuts the zig-zags the road has to take to climb the pass. Do not fail to stop to look behind you from time to time as you climb — it is an unforgettable sight.

After the rugged isolation of the Richetlipass, the Klausenpass, with its coachbound tourists and tacky souvenirs, may be a disappointment, but you can quickly make your escape. With the prospect of quite a lot of road walking before you get to Altdorf, there may be a temptation to hitch a ride or catch a bus from the Klausenpass. But this would be a great mistake, for you would miss out on Asch and the Unterschächen valley.

Leave the road at the pass and follow the sign to Äsch just beyond the kiosks. The path leads gently down a grassy hillside in between the road and a small bach. You should aim for some farm buildings marked on the map as Unter Balm. Cross the bach shortly before getting to them and then, as the view over the magnificent Unterschächen valley unfolds before you, take the track which slithers down below the cliffs to your left.

The way down is a tortuous zig-zag path which is very steep and scree-covered. There has been some attempt to engineer the path and there are wooden railings for some of the way down. It is quite a hazardous descent, but the reward at the bottom is Äsch — surely one of the places on the APR most worthy of the description 'idyllic'. The village is a small agricultural settlement where cattle wander freely around the houses, where there are no roads and the few cars owned by its inhabitants are parked some way away at the end of the track from Unterschachen.

From Äsch, the path to Unterschächen is a pleasant track sloping gently down the valley. Join the road and then almost immediately leave it again to take the final trackway across some fields to Unterschächen. On the left you will see the spectacular Gross Ruchen and Gross Windgallen in the background, through a gap in between the Stuttlisalp and Waspen in the foreground.

The journey from Unterschächen to Altdorf is about 90 per cent road walking, following the line of the Schachen river. Do not attempt to find the track marked on the map as running to the south of the river about one kilometre downstream from Unterschächen — it's not there. Further west, you can leave the road at Spiringen for about one kilometre, but you rejoin it at Witerschwanden.

After this, the Altdorf valley gradually comes into view and the first outskirts of it you come to are at Bürglen, reputedly the home town of William Tell. Altdorf is, aesthetically at least, the low point of the APR and you may want to get through it as fast as possible. A judicious route through the backstreets (possible to navigate with the map) will skirt you round the town centre and probably save you time. But if you are stopping for the night, it might be as well to look for accommodation in Bürglen or Schattdorf rather than crossing to Attinghausen on the western side of the valley floor. There is neither an official campsite nor a youth hostel at Altdorf.

Altdorf is the capital of the Canton of Uri and plays heavily, as far as tourists are concerned, on its association with William Tell. It is supposed to be the place where Herr Tell shot at the apple on his son's head and there is a Tell monument and a Tell theatre where Schiller's 'William Tell' is performed. Other tourist attractions include the Rathaus (Town Hall), the Parish Church of St Martin, the Uri Historical Museum, the Suvorov House and the Capuchin Friary.

Accommodation: Three of the town's cheaper hotels are: Schwarzer Lowen (Tel. 2 10 07) — 32 francs for a single person's room without a shower. Bauernhof (Tel. 2 12 37) — 25-27 francs for a single person's room without a shower. Bahnhof (Tel. 2 10 32) — 23-25 francs for a single person's room without a shower.
These are official quoted prices valid until November 30 1983.

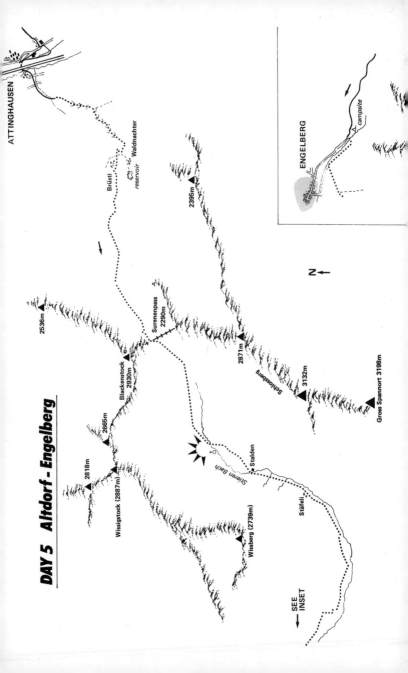

DAY 5 Altdorf - Engelberg

ATTINGHAUSEN

Brüsti
Waldnachter
reservoir

2536m

Surenenpass
2290m

Blackenstock
2930m

2665m

2818m

Wissigstock (2887m)

2871m

3132m

Schlossberg

Gross Spannort 3198m

Wissberg (2739m)

Stieren Bach

Stalden

Stäfeli

SEE
INSET

N

ENGELBERG

campsite

Day 5

Altdorf — Surenenpass — Engelberg
23km/14 miles (7 hours)

Terrain: *A hard day's walk, with a steep climb from Altdorf, then a more gradual ascent to the pass. Pleasant walk down into Engelberg.*
Altitude: *Altdorf (458m). Surenenpass (2291m). Engelberg (1004m).*
Maps: *Sheet 246 Klausenpass, Sheet 245 Stans.*
Views: *The Waldnacht Valley. The Stotziberggrat.*

The way out of the unlovely Altdorf valley is via Attinghausen on the west bank of the Reuss River. However you choose to get through the valley from the east — and there seems to be no direct route from Burglen — you must aim for a small road connecting the road running parallel with the railway line and Attinghausen. This road runs under the railway line, under the motorway and over the river, all within the space of a few hundred metres.

There is a bar conveniently placed on your right after you have crossed the river and it may be worthwhile refuelling there before starting the long climb (about 1,000m) to Waldnachter. Follow the yellow signs from the bridge at Attinghausen pointing towards the Surenenpass. Take the metalled road up through the town and find a narrow cobbled path with stone walls on both sides, leading up through some meadows. The cobblestones end quite soon and the path becomes a steep zig-zag woodland track with a relentless gradient all the way to Waldnacht.

When you finally reach the top of this part of the climb to the pass you will see the astonishing upper valley of Waldnacht below you. It is almost oasis-like in its tranquility after the brutal steepness of the mountain you have just climbed. If you are camping, it is the ideal place to spend the night as there are plenty of level grassy areas to put up a tent around the small reservoir near the small farming settlement of Waldnachter. You should be able to obtain milk and/or cheese from one of the farms.

Even if you are not stopping here you will want to rest at the entrance to the valley before resuming the climb — more gradual now — to the Surenenpass whose awesome prospect is visible from the end of the valley. From the top of the path from Altdorf, do not go down towards the farms, but follow the yellow sign to Brusli leading up the hill to the right. If you have stayed the night at Waldnacht, you will obviously have to retrace your steps to this path.

Go through the unlikely isolated settlement of Brusli with its tiny cable car and along the well-trodden path which roughly follows the ridge along the northern side of the Waldnacht valley. You may find snow on the final approach to the pass but by this time the pass itself will be obvious and you will be able to see the best way of getting across the final valley.

The route down from the Surenenpass is an easy stroll through magnificent mountain scenery. The path passes a small farmhouse which sells drinks (non-alcoholic) and you can sit outside sipping your 'Kalte Ovo' (cold Ovaltine) whilst admiring the extraordinary rock 'amphitheatre' of the Stotziberggrat. Cross the Stieren Bach near the farm and continue downstream to recross it at Stalden. Shortly after this the path forks. You should take the left fork, leading back down towards the river which you follow all the way down into Engelberg.

About two kilometres from Stalden, the inn at Stafeli is a good place to stop for refuelling whilst sitting outside on the terrace admiring the scenery. From here it is an easy walk down into Engelberg, but be sure to stay on the northern side of the river which by now has become the Engelberger.

Engelberg is basically a tourist town with all the usual Swiss sophistication to comfort you if you need a break from the wilderness. In sharp contrast to both the earthiness of your Alpine walk and the flashiness of Engelberg's tourist facilities, the Benedictine church, attached to the monastery a little above the town centre, is a beauty of civilisation. It was founded in 1120 and its abbots exercised ecclesiastical rule over the valley until 1798. The interior of the church is ornate, but light and joyful, lacking the austerity of some other Protestant places of worship. It was designed by Kaspar Moosbrugger and rebuilt in the 1730s after a fire. It has a rich library where men only are admitted, and which contains some valuable manuscripts.

The town has both a youth hostel and an official campsite. Unofficial campsites may be found on the way down into the town in the woods on either side of the Engelberger river.

Accommodation: Cheaper Hotels — Stop (Tel. 94 16 74); Belmont (Tel. 94 24 23); Matter (Tel. 94 15 55); Cathrin Garni (Tel. 94 28 39). Prices for a single room without a shower range between 25 and 45 francs.

DAY 6 Engelberg - Meiringen

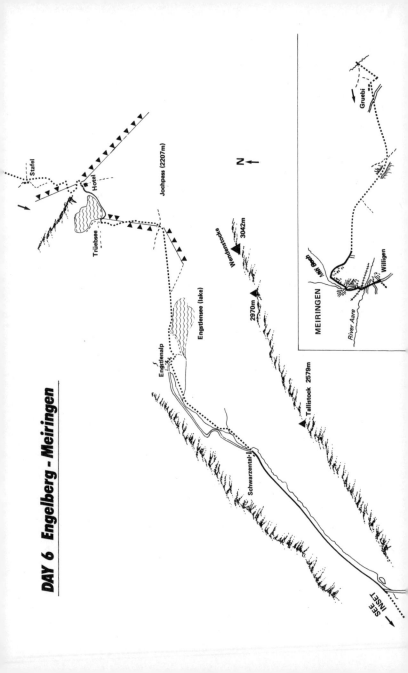

Day 6

Engelberg — Jochpass — Meiringen
28 km/17½ miles (8 hours)

Terrain: *Reasonable climb to the Jochpass. Then a long gradual downhill to Meiringen.*
Altitude: *Engelberg (1004m). Jochpass (2207m). Meiringen (595m).*
Maps: *Sheet 245 Stans, Sheet 255 Sustenpass.*
Views: *The Engstlensee from above.*

From the centre of Engelberg there are various bridges across the river which runs along the south side of the town. If you have stayed at the campsite on the eastern side of the town, you can cross via a footbridge just by it. From the campsite, walk downstream for a few hundred metres and then follow the sign to the Jochpass up through the woods. Before your heart sinks at the thought of another endless uphill grind reminiscent of the climb from Altdorf, take heed that this one does not last for long and you soon find yourself in a pleasant gently-sloping Alpine meadow. Wander past some farm buildings and begin the zig-zag climb to the Trübsee.

This is a pleasant but at times irritating walk, as the zig-zag has been constructed to keep the gradient as gentle as possible and it sometimes seems as if you are not gaining any height at all. Still, the ease of the climb means you have no wish to be travelling in one of the cable cars humming not far above you on their way to the Trübsee hotel.

Which is where the APR momentarily loses every bit of wilderness credibility, for the path, having finally gained some height, leads right into what seems to be the backyard of the Trübsee hotel. You may have to pick your way round empty beer crates and Japanese tourists who have just got off the cable car from Engelberg, but you should be able to swallow your disdain for all this along with the beer which is available on the large hotel terrace.

Go round the front of the hotel and along the concrete path which leads along the side of the Trübsee itself. You walk along this flat upper valley for a short way and then leave the concrete at the southern end of the lake.

If the cable car to the hotel made you wonder why you insisted on doing things the hard way, the final climb to the Jochpass almost allows you to take the easy way out. There is a chairlift whirring away just above your head not far out of arm's reach.

It is a straightforward climb up the line of the lift to the pass which, it must be said, is not much less touristy than the hotel. There are two winding stations there and some kind of restaurant. It is well-worth pausing to take a look at the magnificent range of mountains to the south, including the Reissend Nollen, the Wendenstock and the Mahren.

From the pass follow the path gently downhill towards Engstlenalp and Meiringen. Soon, the spectacular Engstlensee comes into view. If the weather is fine this may be one of the most memorable sights of your trip. The lake reflects the deep cloudless blue of the sky, the grassy mountainside is filled with flowers and overlooking it all is a great mountain ridge flecked with snow. To make claims for the superiority of one vista over another amongst this extravaganza of natural beauty may seem a little superfluous, but the Engstlensee is particularly lovely.

The track levels out as it nears the small settlement of Engstlenalp. Leave the lakeside about half-way along its northern bank and you will shortly come into a settlement which is, among other things, the end of the line for the local post bus.

The footpath to Meiringen starts where the bus stops and winds gently down through open woodland roughly parallel to a bach. You should be able to see the mighty Wetterhorn to the east from this track. After two to three kilometres, you will be walking directly below huge cliffs with glacier water pouring from their sides.

The path runs more or less parallel to the road from Engstlenalp to Meiringen and you should aim to keep off this for as long as possible. However, Meiringen is at least three hours away and you may need to take the most direct route.

To do this, cross the river at Schwarzental and follow the road for about three-and-a-half-kilometres. Look out for a sign saying 'Meiringen 3 Std.' to your right shortly after passing a small lake on the lefthand side of the road.

Between here and Meiringen, the APR becomes a little approximate, as there are a number of footpaths leading along the wooded mountainside above Innertkirchen and Willigen and none seems to be a definitive route to Meiringen. Navigation here needs some care or you can find yourself descending towards the Aare valley too soon.

Go through the tiny settlement marked on the map as Greubi and shortly afterwards hit a road leading up the mountainside from Wyler. Leave it again within a few hundred metres, going off into the woods on your left. Follow the contours around the mountain above Innertkirchen until you are heading in a rough north-westerly direction. Take care here, for the ground is precipitous and the footpath, though roughly level, is very narrow. The route is fairly well-marked with red and white markers. Finally down, mostly through woods, to a residential road on the east side of Meiringen. Follow this up to the Mili Bach where you turn left and follow the bach into the centre of the town.

Camping: There is a site at the north-west end of the town in a field next to the railway line. You need to walk about one kilometre to get there.

Accommodation: Meiringen's cheap hotels include: Hirschen, Bergrestaurant and Restaurant Aareschlucht. Prices for a room without a shower range from 18 to 40 francs with a supplementary charge of between 10 and 20 francs. Meiringen also has a Youth Hostel.

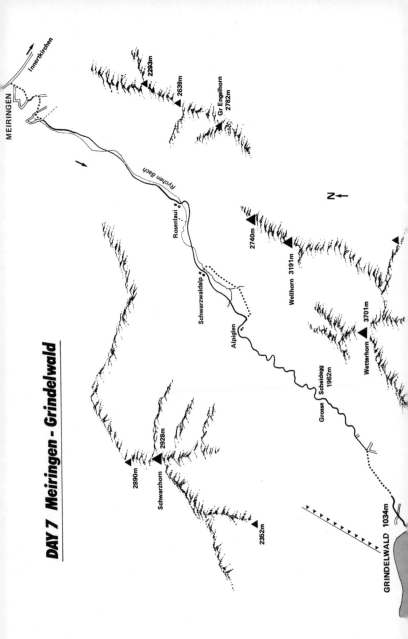

DAY 7 Meiringen - Grindelwald

MEIRINGEN

Innertkirchen

Rychen Bach

Rosenlaui

Schwarzwaldalp

Alpiglen

2293m

2639m

Gr Engelhorn 2782m

2740m

Wellhorn 3191m

Wetterhorn 3701m

Grosse Scheidegg 1962m

N

2890m

Schwarzhorn 2928m

2352m

GRINDELWALD 1034m

Day 7

Meiringen — Grosse Scheidegg — Grindelwald
25km/15 miles (7½ hours)

Terrain: *No severe gradients. A fair amount of road walking, but on minor mountain roads.*
Altitude: *Meiringen (595m). Grosse Scheidegg (1962m). Grindelwald (1034m).*
Maps: *Sheet 255 Sustenpass, Sheet 254 Interlaken.*
Views: *The Grindelwald valley including the Wetterhorn and the Eiger.*

From the centre of Meiringen, cross the Aare going south and walk a short way along the main road to Innertkirchen. Follow the yellow signs towards the Grosse Scheidegg which you should pick up as soon as you walk out of town. Turn right up the hill across a field and through some woods until you hit a small road running along the hillside. Follow this a short way then leave it to go through some woods to join the small mountain road which leads up to the Grosse Scheidegg.

Once on this road, your navigational problems disappear for the day and you can swing along enjoying the ever-present sound of rushing water and the magnificent Wetterhorn getting ever closer. Rosenlaui is a good place for a rest before the road rises more steeply to the pass.

This mountain road is metalled all the way up and carries some traffic, so it is best to use the footpaths which take a more direct route to the top, cutting off many of the sharp bends in the road. At Schwarzwaldalp, you can take a short but scenic detour by turning left off the road, over a stream and along the base of the Kleine Wellhorn to rejoin the road a little way down from Alpiglen.

From the Grosse Scheidegg — ironically named because it is some 100 metres lower than its sister the Kleine Scheidegg — you have an extraordinary view of some of the most famous Alpine scenery in Switzerland.

The Wetterhorn, which you have had in your sights for the last two days, now towers above you; the broad lush valley of Grindelwald stretches below and to its south stands the Eiger. With the possible exception of the Matterhorn, this is Switzerland's most famous — and certainly most notorious mountain. Its north face has been a challenge to climbers for many years, has claimed the lives of some of them and still remains a challenge to many more. One of the most famous accounts of an assault on the north face — Heinrich Harrer's 'The White Spider' is much in evidence on Grindelwald's bookstalls.

However, you can view it from a safe distance, can appreciate its beauty and like the other famous landmarks in the Bernese Oberland, actually be a part of the picture postcard landscape which is unfolding before you.

But no postcard of Switzerland is complete without its cluster of houses nesting cosily in a fertile green valley — and that is where you are heading. Grindelwald fits the bill perfectly and has been doing so for travellers and climbers for many years. Due to its position below the Eiger and the Wetterhorn and in the midst of a lush valley, it has become one of Switzerland's most famous tourist magnets and its setting is one of the most photographed in the country.

You only have to stand by the Grindelwald railway station on a summer's morning to appreciate the popularity of the place. Tourists pour off the trains and wander through the town, taking advantage of the many terrace cafes, souvenir shops and restaurants. The less-desirable trappings of tourism are well-known but somehow the Swiss have avoided them in Grindelwald and while the centre of it seethes with postcards and Pentaxes, its beauty has not been impaired. The walker looking down on the town from either of the Scheidegg passes sees only a small town built in traditional Swiss style spreading along one side of a wide green valley.

Navigation from the Grosse Scheidegg is no problem as

you have Grindelwald in your sights the whole way down. You cannot fail to notice the Upper Glacier on your left as you descend.

One of the more remarkable features of Grindelwald and the surrounding area is its mountain railway network by which you can ascend the Kleine Scheidegg, take a trip to Lauterbrunnen and even climb most of the way up the Jungfrau. But for the climb to the Kleine Scheidegg at least, the hardy walker has no need of wheeled transport.

Camping: The town has two official campsites.

Accommodation: There are many hotels in Grindelwald and many of them are well-endowed with stars. But for the traveller wanting more modest accommodation there are some which fall into the 25-40-francs-a-night price range. These include the Blumlisalp (Tel. 53 13 68); the Panorama (Tel. 53 20 10); the Wetterhorn (Tel. 53 12 18) and the Waldran. There is also a Youth Hostel.

DAY 8 Grindelwald - Lauterbrunnen

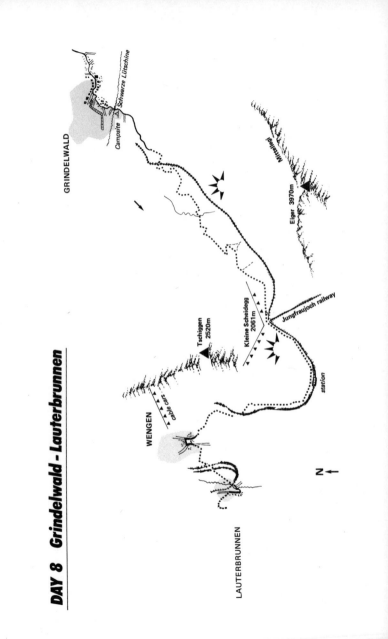

Day 8

Grindelwald — Kleine Scheidegg — Lauterbrunnen
21km/13 miles (5 hours)

Terrain: *Steep but well-surfaced climb out of Grindelwald. Winding forest track then gradual path to Lauterbrunnen. All of it well-trodden.*
Altitude: *Grindelwald (1034m). Kleine Scheidegg (2061m). Lauterbrunnen (795m).*
Map: *Sheet 254 Interlaken.*
Views: *The Eiger and the Jungfrau from the Kleine Scheidegg.*

Do not be deceived by the 'little Scheidegg'. You have to climb more than 3,000ft to get there and the initial stages out of Grindelwald are steep. From the centre of Grindelwald, head south over the river at the bridge where there is a campsite on the south bank. A small metalled road turns into an unmade forest track after about two kilometres and winds up the side of the mountain, crossing the railway line once.

The gradient to the Kleine Scheidegg should present no problems. About one kilometre before the pass itself, you come out of the woods and pass through some pasture land with the Eiger towering right over you. The path is extremely well-trodden, but not so well-travelled, you may be sure, as the railway which shares your destination.

At the risk of a dubious comparison, the Kleine Scheidegg seems like the Venice of the Alps — very beautiful but over-populated with visitors. Its position as a station on the Jungfraujoch railway and its spectacular situation below both the Eiger and the Jungfrau means it rivals even Grindelwald for tourist credibility. The difference is that in the valley town people live and work and did so before tourism began. Here the tourists are all.

You can sit at the large terrace cafe at the pass and watch the little Swiss flags flapping in the breeze, watch the tourists pouring off the train from Lauterbrunnen and maybe even listen to the periodical honking of a caricature Alpenhorn being blown to summon not cattle but tourists.

But before your 'real traveller's' disdain gets the better of you, it may be worth swallowing your pride and taking a trip on the Jungfraujoch Railway, the highest in Europe and the third highest in the world. The journey to the 'joch' or saddle between the Jungfrau and the Monch will take about an hour. Three-quarters of it is through an extraordinary tunnel cut through the Monch, with galleries through which you get amazing glimpses of the great glaciers and of the Wetterhorn, Schreckhorner and Fiescherhorner. The railway finally emerges at some 11,000ft into an extraordinary complex including an hotel, shops, a post office and even a skating rink.

Back down to the Kleine Scheidegg and off down to Lauterbrunnen, although by this time you will have got off the train and be walking easily down the well-trodden path to Wengen. The path roughly follows the railway line taking a steady gradient down the mountain.

Follow the signs to Lauterbrunnen from Wengen, crossing the railway line on the outskirts of the village a little way below a church. The path then descends quite steeply through fields and then woods to Lauterbrunnen.

Lauterbrunnen lies in a spectacular narrow valley which, like Grindelwald and the Kleine Scheidegg, is one of the major tourist attractions of the Bernese Oberland. This valley boasts some spectacular waterfalls which pour down the steep cliff sides of the valley. One of the two largest is the Staubbach which has a drop of more than 900ft and can be seen from one of the campsites on the outskirts of the town.

Lauterbrunnen is in some ways the culmination of the Bernese Oberland section of the APR. It is your last stopping point in this famous area of the Eiger, the Wetterhorn and the Jungfrau. If you are getting tired of rubbing shoulders with other kinds of tourists you may be relieved to know that the route from here is decidedly less populated — with the possible exception of Mürren, your next port of call. But while you are staying in Lauterbrunnen you must share the place with the coach parties, and there are plenty of these.

Camping: There are two official campsites in Lauterbrunnen.

Accommodation: Three of the cheaper hotels in Lauterbrunnen are: the Sternen (Tel. 55 12 31); the Baren (Tel. 55 16 34); and the Kaufman (Tel. 55 17 23).

DAY 9 *Lauterbrunnen – Griesalp*

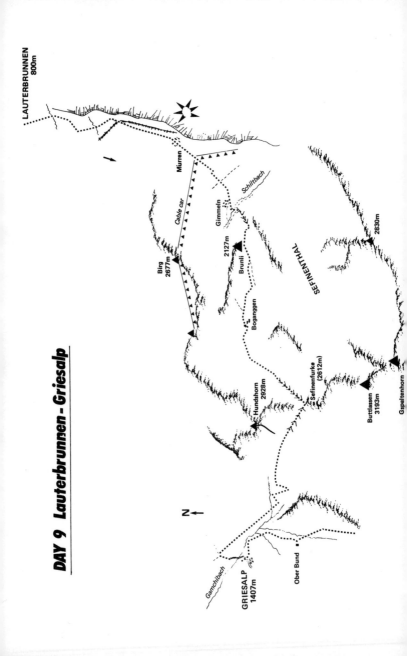

LAUTERBRUNNEN 800m

Mürren

Cable car

Birg 2677m

Gimmeln

Schiltbach

Brunli 2127m

Boganggen

SEFINENTHAL

2830m

Hundshorn 2928m

Sefinenfurke (2612m)

Buttlassen 3193m

Gspaltenhorn

N

Garnchibach

GRIESALP 1407m

Ober Bund

Day 9

Lauterbrunnen — Mürren — Sefinenfurke
— Griesalp
23km/14½ miles (9 hours)

Terrain: *Hard. Two major climbs with a combined ascent of nearly 2,000m. Pleasant but sometimes steep woodland track up to Mürren. Mostly gradual gradients then until the final approach to the Sefinenfurke, the steepest climb on the APR. A long descent to Griesalp sometimes made difficult by scree.*
Altitude: *Lauterbrunnen (795m). Mürren (1645m). Sefinenfurke (2612m). Griesalp (1407m).*
Maps: *Sheet 254 Interlaken, Sheet 264 Jungfrau.*
Views: *Eiger, Monch and Jungfrau from Mürren. Blumlisalp from Sefinenfurke.*

The path to Mürren is signposted leading up the hill in the midst of Lauterbrunnen's main street. There is a steep climb up a concrete path for a short way and then into the woods which continue most of the way up to Mürren. The path climbs more gradually as you get towards the village and it makes a delightful woodland walk, with streams rushing under the track and occasional glimpses of the Lauterbrunnen valley seemingly miles below. Through the trees you can also see the Jungfrau, making this path one of the most photogenic stretches of the APR.

Suddenly you are out of the trees and crossing the railway track on its final approach to Mürren, the highest village in the Bernese Oberland. As you stroll the final few hundred yards into the village, it becomes clear why it has — even in such a paradise — a reputation for its magnificent scenery. The scenery in view at this moment is the extraordinary triptych of the Jungfrau, the Monch and further to the east, the Eiger which seems to have been marking your progress for the last three days. I long ago ran out of fresh superlatives for describing the scenery on this route, but it is at this point that it seems to acquire a majesty it did not have before and you get the feeling you are ascending into some very special high country.

Cross the railway line and stroll down the path beside it into the village. Take the opportunity of having a beer at one of the cafes there and take in the view, for while you have not reached the highest point on the APR yet and there is still much memorable country to pass through, there is something special about this.

When you can drag yourself away, continue through the town, past the Schilthorn cable car station and take a farm track up the hill to Schonegg and Gimmeln. When you get to the farm settlement of Gimmeln, turn left off the main track, wander past a farm and down the hill to cross the Schiltbach. Do not be tempted to turn right after you have crossed it in order to follow the track which leads up the mountain next to it. You should head roughly south for a short distance to find a well-trodden track which winds steeply up the side of a mini-summit called Brunli.

Once you have climbed most of Brunli, you have a very restful walk along the contours, passing through pleasant green mountainside which could almost be English moorland. About two-and-a-half kilometres after ascending Brunli, you come to Boganggen, a small farmstead which lies at the end of a rock-strewn valley, is within sight of the Schilthorn and, most importantly, sells beer. The owners evidently run some kind of guest house for trekkers and climbers during the summer months, but you should not count on getting accommodation there. Boganngen is, however, a good place to camp if you are running out of time or energy or find the prospect of the Sefinenfurke too much to face that day. There is plenty of flat grass to pitch your tent and a good water supply.

If you are more interested in the beer supply, it is worth noting a few things about Swiss beer if you have not found them out already. It is a subject likely to be of some concern during your trip, especially if the weather is hot. Commonly-available Swiss beer falls into the category English real ale buffs would call Eurofizz. It is usually light, fizzy lager, served cold and in bottles. It is very good for thirst-quenching and possibly even better than water, for it may help replace the odd body salt as well as the fluid. Being light, it is also unlikely to stop you in your tracks for the rest of the day, providing, of course, it is taken in reasonable quantities. The various brands are all much of a muchness, with the dramatic exception of 'alkoholfreibiere' which can give you a nasty shock. Some cafes serve this automatically if you ask for beer, simply because they don't serve the real thing. It is fine, of course, if you are teetotal, but if not it may come as a rude awakening to English palates.

From Boganggen, walk to the western end of the rock-strewn valley and then follow the track in a south-westerly direction at a fairly easy gradient up towards the Sefinen-furke.

The final climb to the Sefinenfurke looks like a sheer wall as you approach and it is not far off that. It is one of the few times you will have to scramble rather than walk, and its ascent is a matter of getting to the top as best you can, for the soft scree does not allow any proper path to stay in place. From the top, just a narrow ridge of rock, you can see the Blumlisalp, including the Hohtürli, the highest pass on the APR.

Take care on the way down from the pass as you have to cross steep scree for about one kilometre before the ground gets less steep. The path down to Griesalp follows a stream for a way and shortly before you leave it, you will come to the farm of Ober Durrenberg where you can buy refreshments such as cold Ovaltine. Cross the stream by that farm and continue down the mountain through pastures and, later, woods. Do not follow a sign to the Hohtürli on your left as you near Griesalp.

The main part of the village of Griesalp clusters round the hotel by the Gamchibach, but before you descend into the valley, you pass a shop on the left. In summer 1982 this appeared to be the only place to obtain supplies.

Camping: There is no official campsite at Griesalp.

Accommodation: There is one hotel in Griesalp, the Kurhaus Griesalp (Tel. 76 12 31).

Day 10

Griesalp — Hohtürli — Kandersteg
16km/10 miles (6 hours)

Terrain: *A constant climb, very steep at the end, to the highest point of the APR. Gradient not too severe until the last two kilometres before the pass. After the pass a long but steady descent past the Oeschinensee to Kandersteg.*
Altitude: *Griesalp (1407m). Hohtürli (2778m). Kandersteg (1176m).*
Maps: *Sheet 264 Jungfrau, Sheet 263 Wildstrubel.*
Views: *From the Hohtürli in all directions. The Oeschinensee from the track above it.*

The path to the Hohtürli is clearly signposted near the Griesalp Hotel. Walk through woodland roughly parallel to the Gamchlibach for about one kilometre and then turn southwards to climb more steeply. Soon you have a tributary of the Gamchlibach, the Bundbach, to guide you up the mountain.

Keep to the west side of the Bundbach and come to the tiny settlement of Ober Bund where there is a farm and some kind of guest house where you can buy refreshments.

If you are pausing for the night — and this is only possible if you are camping — before climbing the Hohtürli, the area of Ober Bund is a good place to stop, with gently-sloping mountainside, plenty of fresh water and magnificent views.

From Ober Bund you must cross the Bundbach to its eastern side and after about half-a-kilometre you start the really serious climb of the Hohtürli. The path makes no concessions to the faint-hearted and cuts at brutal right angles across the contours. With the pass about one kilometre distant, the gradient moderates somewhat and goes

DAY 10 Griesalp - Kandersteg

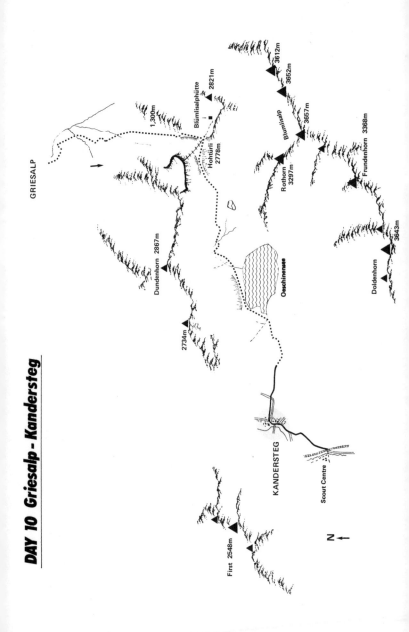

GRIESALP

1,300m

Blümlisalphütte 2821m

Hohtürli 2778m

3612m

3652m

Blümlisalp 3657m

Rothorn 3297m

Frundenhorn 3368m

Dundenhorn 2867m

2734m

3643m

Doldenhorn

Oeschinensee

First 2548m

KANDERSTEG

Scout Centre

N

towards a rocky ridge which can provide a welcome respite before the final assault on the pass.

Briefly savour the sight of the valley below and then make your way directly below the ridge on its eastern side over the last half-a-kilometre to the pass itself. You will have earned a good rest by the time you get here and fortunately there is a bit more room on the pass than on the razor edge of the Sefinenfurke.

If you have the energy, an extra couple of hundred feet will take you to the Blumlisalphutte just above the pass where food and accommodation is available, but drinking water is evidently — and understandably — in short supply. The hut is run by the Swiss Alpine Club.

The way down to Kandersteg is steep and scree-ridden at first and should be taken carefully. Follow a ridge for about one kilometre and then a series of rocky paths. As the ground levels out somewhat, you follow for about half-a-kilometre a small stream, first on its northern and then on its southern bank. Suddenly the track veers steeply away and there is the Oeschinensee. This large lake has been obscured until now from your line of vision, but dramatically this vast body of water appears before you and hundreds of feet below.

Leave the stream you have been following (staying with it will result in an unwelcomely fast drop down a precipice) and climb down the cliff track leading towards the edge of the lake. Parts of this track have cables held into the rock to help you down. As the track descends and approaches the lake, you have a wonderful view of the cliffs on its south-eastern side. Walk along the north side of the lake beneath a spectacular overhang and down through some woods to the very touristy restaurant/hotel at its western end. Be warned that this place is very expensive, even for small refreshments and, in summer 1982, was one of the pernicious purveyors of the aforementioned biere sans alcool.

More acceptable refreshments are available in Kandersteg which is only about 30 minutes away down a gently-sloping track. Kandersteg is a pleasant tourist town renowned for its links with the scouting movement. At the southern end of the town — and on your way to the Bunderchrinde tomorrow — is the International Scout Centre where uniformed youngsters from all over the world put up tents, build wobbly rope bridges and mount expeditions.

Camping: There are two official sites in Kandersteg. If you are looking for unofficial sites, it would be as well to try on the south side of the town, in the direction you will be travelling tomorrow. Turn left on to Kandersteg's main street when you come off the track from the Oeschinensee. Walk more or less parallel to the railway for about one kilometre. After this, the road and the railway converge and the road goes underneath. Go under the bridge and turn right immediately afterwards. The Scout Centre is immediately in front of you. Cross over the fast-flowing River Kander and turn immediately left rather than going down into the Scout Centre. Now on a footpath, pass some farm buildings on your right and cross a field between two fences. Continue in a roughly south-westerly direction for a few hundred metres, passing some cliffs to your right. Follow roughly the line of cliffs to the corner of the field where the woods begin. Here you will find a yellow sign to the Bunderchrinde. The field you have just crossed may be a suitable area for pitching a tent.

Accommodation: Kandersteg's cheaper hotels include: the National (Tel. 75 14 84); the Simplon (Tel. 75 11 73): the Bahnhof Buffet (Tel. 75 13 50); and the Rendez-vous (Tel. 75 13 54). Prices range between 25-40 francs per person per night for a room without a shower.

Day 11

Kandersteg — Bunderchrinde — Adelboden
19 km/12 miles (6 hours)

Terrain: *A tough climb from Uschene to the pass. Some parts of the path are very steep and there is a lot of scree over the last half kilometre. Loose scree also on the first part of the descent from the pass. Otherwise a fairly easy stroll to Adelboden.*
Altitude: *Kandersteg (1176m). Bunderchrinde (2385m). Adelboden (1348m).*
Maps: *Sheet 263 Wildstrubel.*
Views: *Eastwards from the Bunderchrinde and from the track on the way up.*

From the corner of the field described in the Camping section at the end of yesterday's walk, head up through the woods. You soon cross the road which zig-zags up to the Uschene valley. You can cut these zig-zags by walking through the woods for a certain distance but you will eventually have to follow the road until it levels out into the upper valley. Do not be tempted to follow any track which leads up besides the rushing Alpbach even if there are signs pointing that way. A track which leads along the river's banks only peters out and you would be forced to climb steeply to get back on the road.

Follow the road west as it levels out in the picturesque upper valley of Uschene. Pass a junction with a road coming in from your right and go past a couple of farm buildings. Follow a sign up a path which turns right off the road and begin to climb the Bunderchrinde.

This is the last typical high Alpine pass you will climb and the views are fittingly wonderful. A couple-of-hundred-metres from the valley floor the track does a dog-leg and

DAY 11 Kandersteg - Adelboden

turns for a short time away from the direction of the pass. Shortly, resume climbing straight up and, once over a ridge, more or less follow the contours below the ridge of the three Lohner peaks.

Be careful to take the left fork at the farm below the pass and then follow the winding path over grassland and then scree to the pass. The final approach to the pass is made from a north-easterly direction, climbing diagonally across a scree slope. Due to the angle of your approach, it is difficult to judge exactly where the pass is as you get near it and it may come as a pleasant surprise when you find you are nearer the top than you thought.

The Bunderchrinde does not have the same feeling of ruggedness and isolation as some of the passes you have crossed, but it is a marvellous place all the same. To the west you can look down and almost see Adelboden, and to the east you can say a final farewell to the mountains of the Bernese Oberland. To have thought it was all down-hill from the Hohtürli would not have allowed for the Bunderchrinde, but now you have climbed that, you will enter more gentle country whose character contrasts sharply with the dramatic sights of the Eiger and the Jungfrau.

Navigation from the pass to Adelboden should present no problems. Take care on the initial scree slope, but after this the route is straightforward and the path is well-trodden. As you make your way out of the U-shaped valley bounded by the Bunderspitz on one side and the Numih on the other, pause to look back where you have just come and you will see the Bunderchrinde as an obvious 'bite' out of the rock ridge which looks down on you.

As you leave the valley, you pass a large number of piles of rock which lie there as if someone had been sweeping up the valley floor and had not got around to disposing of the debris. Refreshments are available at a little inn at Chumi on the way down, but once again it is an alcoolfreihaus and even says so on the eves. Much of the rest of the day's walk is down a small mountain road which winds through woodland towards the Bunderle Bach. The road does a dog-leg here and continues its descent into Adelboden, passing increasing numbers of houses as it does so. Go down into the town and cross the river on to the main road running along the valley floor.

Having crossed the bridge at the bottom of the road from the pass, turn left and walk along the main road for about half-a-kilometre until you come to a soft drinks factory on your left. There is a hairpin bend in the road here, leading up to Adelboden town centre. Leave the main road and walk along the smaller one running past the factory. It runs down to the Allebach which you cross and re-cross to walk along its north side for a short way. On that bank, near the point where the path meets the road coming down from the town centre, there is a little shelter where you can drink from a sulphur spring. If you thought alcohol free beer was bad, try this. You are now in the area on the west side of the town which seems less populated and fairly well-wooded and likely to be suitable for camping.

Adelboden is a pleasant town, but obviously tourist-based to its roots. One gets the impression that it operates at only half throttle during the summer months and exists mainly for the influx of skiers in winter. It has a number of extremely old chalets and a 14th century church containing a fine 16th century fresco of the Last Judgement.

Camping: There are two official campsites in Adelboden. One is the Ruedy Huss (Tel. 033 73 14 54) and the other the Albo (Tel. 033 73 12 09). Unofficial sites could be difficult to find and it probably pays to head towards the west side of the town (as described above), having the added advantage of putting the odd kilometre behind you before tomorrow has even started.

Accommodation: Adelboden has a fair selection of un-starred hotels which may be of interest to the walker. These include: the Engstligenalp Berghaus (Tel. 73 13 73); the Pension Hari (Tel. 73 19 66); the Pension Alpina (Tel. 73 22 25); the Schonegg, Garni (Tel. 73 16 61). On the way to Lenk you will also find the Hahnenmoospass, Berghotel (Tel. 73 21 41). All these hotels will charge between 30-50 francs per person per night for a room without a shower. There is also a Youth Hostel.

Day 12

Adelboden — Hahnenmoospass — Lenk
16km/11 miles (5 hours)

Terrain: *Not much more than half-a-day's easy walking.
Gentle gradients over road and well-trodden trackway.*
Altitude: *Adelboden (1348m). Hahnenmoospass (1956m).
Lenk (1068m).*
Maps: *Sheet 263 Wildstrubel.*
Views: *The valley of Lenk on the way down from the
Hahnenmoospass.*

From the centre of Adelboden, take the main road west
and cross the Allebach about one kilometre outside the
town centre. Follow the road for about two kilometres
from this. It is evidently the best way to the pass, and
being a small country lane, is very pleasant to walk on. The
road bends to the left when you get to a timber camp and
you should carry straight on, leaving the camp to your left.
You will have a pleasant walk up the side of the Geilsbach
and through some woodland to the hotel/tourist resort of
Geilsbuel. From here it is but a short hop to the pass, although climbing passes seems to have got a bit domestic by
this stage. By now you are a veteran of such gruelling tests
of physical strength and mental determination as the Hohtürli and the Sefinenfurke, so this climb which does not
even reach 2,000m, barely warrants the name 'pass'. What is
more, most people seem to be ascending it in a line of ugly
little red-painted podules which dominate and unfortunately ruin the scene.

    For the hard men and women of the Alpine Pass
Route, with their muscled legs and weather-beaten faces, it
is just a leisurely stroll up to the pass along a winding
metalled road.

DAY 12 Adelboden - Lenk

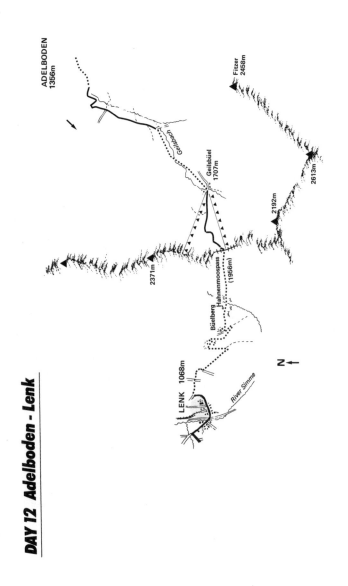

ADELBODEN
1356m

Geilsbach

Geilsbüel
1707m

Fitzer
2458m

2613m

2192m

2371m

Hahnenmoospass
(1956m)

Büelberg

LENK 1068m

River Simme

N

It is a gentle but surprisingly long walk down into Lenk from the pass, the last couple of kilometres being on roads. There are plenty of yellow signposts to guide you down into the town.

Camping: If you are camping, it may be worth, in view of the shortness of today's walk, to put a little more distance behind you and push on towards the Truttlisbergpass. There is plenty of good camping in the woods and pastures of the beautiful Wallbach valley. Lenk has an official campsite — the Hasenweide (Tel. 030 32647).

Accommodation: Lenk is also fairly well-endowed with modest guest houses and hotels. These include: The Hotel Simmenfalle (Tel. 3 10 89); the Zum Gade (Tel. 3 22 33); the Hotel Alpenruh (Tel. 3 10 64); the Pension Edelweiss (Tel. 3 10 65); the Pension Sunnestubli (Tel. 3 28 21); and the Iffigenalp (Tel. 3 13 33).

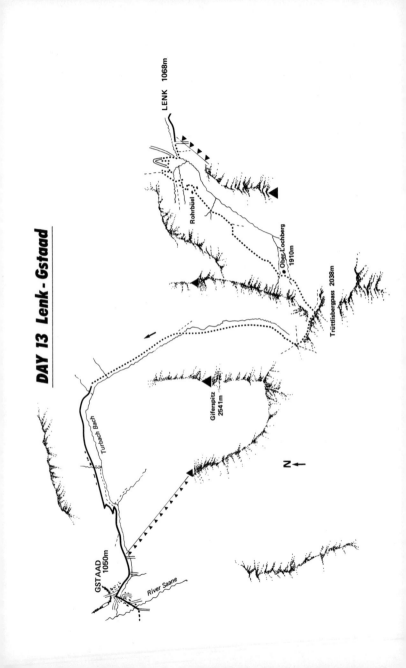

DAY 13 Lenk - Gstaad

LENK 1068m

Rohrbüel

Ober Lochberg
1910m

Trüttlisbergpass 2038m

Giferspitz
2541m

Turbach Bach

GSTAAD
1050m

River Saane

N

Day 13

Lenk — Truttlisbergpass — Gstaad
24km/15 miles (8 hours)

Terrain: *A long climb to the pass, boggy in places. Also a boggy descent into the Turbach valley. From there, a pleasant downhill to Gstaad.*
Altitude: *Lenk (1068m). Truttlisbergpass (2038m). Gstaad (1050m).*
Maps: *Sheet 263 Wildstrubel.*
Views: *The Turbach valley from near the Truttlisbergpass. South-eastwards from the Wallbach valley.*

If you have stayed the night in or around Lenk, it is not difficult to find your way out and up towards the Truttlisbergpass. If you thought the real walking country was behind you in the Bernese Oberland, the Swiss obviously don't, for there is a huge bank of yellow signs in the centre of Lenk, pointing the walker in every conceivable direction, including Gstaad, your destination for the day.

Follow these signs out of town, leaving the municipal swimming pool on your right. Shortly before reaching a small tributary of the River Simme, turn left up a steepish road and into some woods. Cross the stream over a small bridge after about one kilometre and come out of the woods to find yourself on the small, unmade, but car-size road which leads up towards the Truttlisbergpass.

This is a steady climb through woodland and then farmland and the road eventually turns into a footpath. It crosses three small tributaries of the Wallbach. After the third, the path forks and you must take the right fork, climbing up the side of the valley towards the farm at Ober Lochberg.

Now you are in country of quite a different nature from the glamour of the Bernese Oberland. You have left behind the glaciers, snow-capped peaks and great rock precipices and are now in a gentler but no less beautiful environment. Its lack of Eigers could be seen as a recommendation, for the APR west of Lenk is far less well-trodden than the Bernese section and there is a feeling of privilege as you venture deep into some lesser-known country.

The upper valley leading to the Truttlisbergpass is a very beautiful place, consisting mostly of gentle grassy slopes. Pass through a small farm with a well-placed water butt outside. The path is fairly well-trodden along the grassy hillside and, about one kilometre after the last farm, you will find yourself approaching the farm of Ober Lochberg.

Leave the farm to your left and shortly afterwards descend a gully to cross a stream. Take care not to follow the path which leads up the mountain on the north bank of the stream. Once over that stream, roughly follow a ridge for a short way and then follow the 2,000m contour to the Truttlisbergpass itself.

This too is quite a different proposition to previous high passes whether they be jagged gaps in walls of rock or razor edges between two peaks. There is no precipitous climb as the final approach to this and, if there was not a sign to tell you so, you could be forgiven for thinking it was just another grassy hilltop.

In fact, the Truttlisbergpass is the convergence of a number of tracks, all of which, of course, are meticulously signposted. You must turn right here to follow the sign to Gstaad and climb a little to a trig point and then along the side of the mountain with the Lauenen valley far below to your left. After half-a-kilometre, you will find yourself on a saddle between the Truttlisbergpass and the Lauenenehore. From here you will have, assuming the weather is clear, a good view of the Lauenen valley to the east and the more remote Turbach valley to the west.

Head steeply down to your right towards the River Turbach. This hillside drains water from a considerable area into the Turbach and so is very boggy. The path is therefore rather vague for half-a-kilometre or so, on the steepest part of the descent to the river. You should aim for a fairly-well-trodden path leading along the west side of the river and a short distance above it. Follow this for about two kilometres and cross the river at a rough cattle bridge. The valley could be full of cattle, so bear this in mind if you are thinking of camping there. Assuming you can avoid the cattle, though, this place is marvellous for camping — peaceful, well-watered and very beautiful.

The stretch between Lenk and Gstaad may be one of the last chances you have to savour the joys of camping in the Alps and the valleys on either side of the Truttlisberg-pass are idyllic places to stop for the night. Whatever advantages hotels and youth hostels have for the walker, the experience of camping in open countryside after a hard day in the mountains is incomparable. Self-sufficiency is in some ways the hardest way of doing things, but in common with the old adage that you get as much out of something as you put in, the rewards are many. To sit outside your tent, with a stream rushing by and to rest your aching muscles as the sun goes down over the nearest peak, is an experience somehow more appropriate to such a journey as this than surrendering to the soft comforts of a hotel.

From the Turbach valley it is a long and gradual descent to jet-set Gstaad, a place which, as if indicating its affluence, has no official listed campsites. Here you are on the border of the French and German influence in Switzerland and your nearness to the by now Grail-like Montreux is emphasised by the cream and blue trains which pull in at Gstaad station having made the climb from the famous lakeside city. In Gstaad you can sit on one of the terrace cafes and watch the world go by, perhaps hoping to spot a film star or two. Like Adelboden, this place has the feeling of just ticking over during the summer months, preparing to get into top gear when the winter snows bring their coterie of the rich and fashionable to ski and be seen on the slopes.

Camping: No official campsites in Gstaad.

Accommodation: When you survey the famous Gstaad Palace Hotel, with its surfeit of stars, you would think the idea of a cheap hotel in Gstaad was a non-starter. But there are some which may come within the budget of the average APR walker. These include: The Bahnof Garni (Tel. 4 14 22); the Landhaus Kranichhof (Tel. 4 15 25) and the Sonnenhof-Walddorf (Tel. 4 10 23).

Day 14

Gstaad — Col de Jable — L'Etivaz/
La Lecherette
16km/20km/11 miles/12½ miles (6 hours)

Terrain: *Steep climb out of Gstaad, then two further climbs to get to the pass. Descent to L'Etivaz steep in places. All firm underfoot.*
Altitude: *Gstaad (1050m). Col de Jable (1884m). L'Etivaz (1140m). La Lecherette (1379m).*
Maps: *Sheet 263 Wildstrubel; Sheet 262 Rochers de Naye.*
Views: *Eastwards from the Col de Jable.*

The choice of destination on this penultimate day's walk is based on two considerations: the availability of accommodation and the length of the final day's walk to Montreux. The fact that accommodation at both destinations is likely to be limited and that they are within four kilometres of each other suggests that they could be put forward as alternatives. The walk to Montreux tomorrow is not severe and so the 34km journey involved for those who choose to stop at L'Etivaz is not too much to ask. But then you might want to savour those last few miles and by pushing on to La Lecherette tonight you will give yourself a bit more time to enjoy what is a marvellous final day's walk. If you are camping, clearly none of this applies to you. Bear in mind also that accommodation in both these stopping places may not be easy to find.

When you can drag yourself away from Glamorous Gstaad, walk south through the main street, under a railway bridge in the middle of the town and out on the road towards Gsteig. A few hundred metres after crossing the Louibach, leave the main road to take a small residential

DAY 14 Gstaad - L'Etivaz / La Lecherette

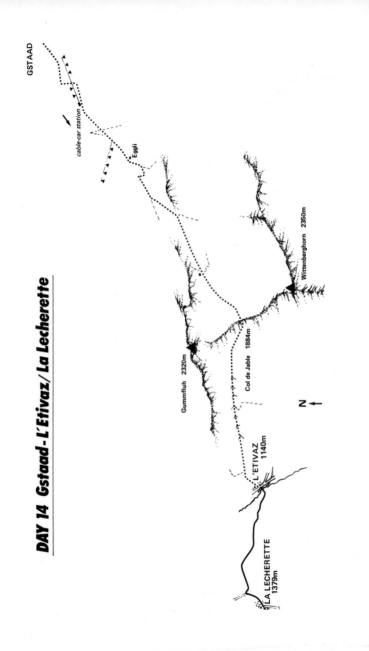

GSTAAD

cable-car station

Eggli

Gummfluh 2320m

Wittenberghorn 2350m

Col de Jable 1884m

N

L'ETIVAZ 1140m

LA LECHERETTE 1379m

road to your right. This takes you over the River Saane and on to a footpath which leads up through some woods. Signposts just as you cross the Saane give you a choice of routes to the Col de Jable, but the one pointing straight on evidently involves a lot more road walking than the one taken here.

Once into the woods there is a very steep climb for a short way and then a walk along the contours followed by an uphill slog for about one kilometre to the top of the cable car run. This provides the same strange feeling as the Jochpass climb all those days ago, when cable cars whir not far above your head laden with people who stare curiously at you wondering why. This experience may produce the same feeling in the walker.

You will need a rest by the time you get to the top, but it is all very touristy and your toil only begins to seem worthwhile when you look over in the direction you are about to travel and see the Col de Jable looking high and isolated.

From the cable car station go down the hill in a south-westerly direction and then up again the other side of a large gully. Follow a ridge over some grassland and then on to a small road which passes, on the left, a new development. Descending from here you see straight in front of you a wooded hill marked on the map as Eggli. The yellow sign at its base tells you the Col de Jable is reached by way of it and so it is that way you must go.

Climbing up Eggli and down the other side is an odd 'first' for the APR for you have to traverse a very narrow and sometimes overgrown footpath over this heavily-wooded hill. Despite the difficulty of the footpath, it is quite distinct and should deliver you, after about one kilometre, back on to farmland on the other side.

From here you have a steady ascent, crossing the contours at only gentle angles to get to the Col de Jable. The path runs through open woodland and pasture and finally past a farm and along a rocky track to climb to the pass itself.

The Col de Jable is a pass in the same tradition as the Truttlisberg — grassy, gentle and undramatic. But its chief significance as far as the APR is concerned is that it marks the barrier between French and German Switzerland. Whatever French influence there may have been in Gstaad, the place is still officially German. A stream there is known as a bach, its suburbs have names like Oberbort and the mountains nearby are called things like Giferspitz. Even the final two kilometres east of the pass are accompanied by the names Lager, Usser and Gumm Matten.

Suddenly it all changes. With daunting Swiss efficiency, the signs, the map names and very soon even the buildings become French and it feels like you are in a different country. As you pass from the Bern to the Vaud canton, the Wanderweg suddenly becomes the Chemin du Pietons, the sign at the pass marks the walking time in heurs and not stunden. And, of course, you are standing at a col rather than a pass.

You have to physically climb over the boundary line between the two cantons — and that is marked by a fence. Follow the sign — just as reliably yellow as its Teutonic counterparts — to L'Etivaz.

The path takes you along the side of the spur of the Gummfluh, rising slightly and then cutting down gradually across the contours above the valley where the tiny village of L'Etivaz lies. You walk through a fair amount of woodland and eventually join a zig-zag track not far above L'Etivaz.

If you had any doubts you were in a different country since crossing the pass, L'Etivaz will dispel them, for it is delightfully French. A roadside cafe (where you may find accommodation) sits by a road junction with a terrace nicely cluttered with red-painted tables and chairs.

If you are continuing to La Lecherette for the night, this unfortunately involves more than three kilometres of road walking, but there appears to be no satisfactory way of travelling west in order to get to the Lac de L'Hongrin — one of tomorrow's attractions. The main feature of La Lecherette is a transport cafe which may provide accommodation. It is the point where you (thankfully) leave the road to wander through some of the APR's most beautiful and isolated countryside. But more of that tomorrow.

Camping: *L'Etivaz:* Official campsites are out of the question in this neck of the woods and unofficial ones are also difficult to come by. With considerable discretion, you might get away with camping by the side of the Tonneresse which flows through the middle of the village, but this will probably involve some fence hopping and should certainly not involve over-staying your welcome. You might do better to press on up the hill towards La Lecherette to look for a place to camp.

La Lecherette: Camping in the vicinity of La Lecherette needs some circumspection, especially bearing in mind local construction work. You might be well-advised to fall a little short of the village and find somewhere to camp in the woods near the road.

Accommodation: This can be possibly found at the roadside cafe in L'Etivaz, or at the transport cafe in La Lecherette.

DAY 15 L'Etivaz/La Lecherette – Montreux

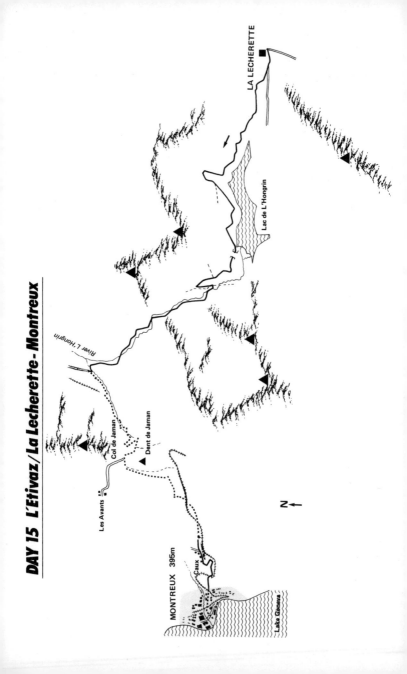

LA LECHERETTE

Lac de L'Hongrin

River L'Hongrin

Les Avants

Col de Jaman

Dent de Jaman

MONTREUX 395m

Caux

Lake Geneva

N

Day 15

L'Etivaz/La Lecherette — Lac de L'Hongrin —
Col de Jaman — Montreux
34/30km/22/19½ miles (9 hours)

Terrain: *Easy but long. Moderate climb to the Col de Jaman. Final descent to Montreux long and tiring.*
Altitude: *L'Etivaz/La Lecherette (1140/1379m). Lac de L'Hongrin (1255m). Col de Jaman (1512m). Montreux (372m).*
Maps: *Sheet 262 Rochers de Naye.*
Views: *The valley of the L'Hongrin river descending from the lake. Lake Geneva (if not obscured by haze) from the Col de Jaman.*

A long day through some wonderful countryside to finish the APR. If you are starting from L'Etivaz you will have a three kilometre walk up the road to La Lecherette. It is a good place to stop for morning coffee/breakfast and sells chocolate and other comestibules to keep your blood sugar up on the way to Montreux.

Turn off the main road you have been walking up and take a small road towards the Lac de L'Hongrin. After a few hundred metres the road forks and you must take the right fork to take you round the north side of the lake. The road stays at some height above the lake — which has been turned into a reservoir — and gives you a wonderful view over this large stretch of water. The unyielding tarmac of the road is a bit hard on the feet after so many days of walking on springy mountain turf, but it is a pleasant walk and there should be very little traffic on the road which takes a good many miles to reach anywhere at all.

Following the north side of the lake you eventually come to the dam and its attendant hydroelectric scheme.

This is a good place for a rest, for you can peer at the huge concrete retaining wall and find out all about the dam and how it generates electricity by reading an enormous display board nearby. Even if you are not interested in hydro-electricity, the board is quite useful for practising your French in preparation for the blow-out you are going to have when you reach Montreux. From here the magical Montreux still seems a long way off, but the display board is a comfort on that score, for it tells you that the power generated there is transmitted to Montreux which, according to the board, is only 10km away.

To continue your journey down the river L'Hongrin you need to go through a short tunnel bored through the cliff right by the dam. You gradually descend into a beautiful valley which, by the standards of the Bernese Oberland, certainly is 'forgotten'. Heavily wooded hills slope down to the small, shallow river besides which, under a canopy of trees, snakes a tiny road, evidently used as much for local agriculture as anything else. There has clearly been no effort to cater for tourists and it would seem unlikely that there ever will be, for there are no obvious attractions there — just its beauty.

All this, and much I have already said, assumes a qualitative judgement about 'tourists' and other types of travellers of whom Alpine Pass Route walkers are a part. Followers of this route are, in one sense, just as much 'tourists' as any other foreign visitors who are spending their holidays looking around another country. This book does not set out to criticise the way many people spend their holidays — of course they should spend them however they choose. But this guide is written on the assumption that its readers will be looking for something in walking the Alpine Pass Route which is not to be found in the postcard shops of Grindelwald or the mountain railways of the Bernese Oberland.

It is a lovely flat, wooded walk along the side of the river L'Hongrin for about five kilometres before turning south-westwards for the final climb of the APR to the Col de Jaman. The turning is made a few hundred metres after a sharp bend in the road where it crosses a small tributary of the main river. By this stage you have just made your way out of the trees and are going into more open country. The left turning, which is marked by a yellow sign to the Col de Jable, is a rough track which leads up the hill gradually at first and then more steeply. Above and to the right, you can see trains about to go through the mountain you are climbing over.

Cross a branch of the main railway line and zig-zag up a farm track. Pass a farm on your right and initially keep to the north of the stream flowing down the valley. But as you ascend, the track, which has been given a gentle gradient by some kind soul, crosses and re-crosses the stream. Your journey up the valley is accompanied by protruding air inlets for the railway tunnel and you can sometimes hear the trains rumbling through the mountain far below. The trek up to the col is not difficult and you should be in reasonable shape for your final triumphant descent to Montreux which is, if anything, more taxing.

From the psychological barrier of this, the final pass of the APR, it is very tempting to think it is but a short hop to Montreux and that the hard work is now over. I'm afraid this is not the case and you should allow for at least two hours' hard walking to get down to the lakeside.

But while you are here, have a beer at the cafe and wander over to the other side of the car park to look, if it is not obscured by haze, at the famous Lake Geneva or Lac Leman. Surveying this view is an act akin to Moses and his followers looking down at the Promised Land. It is a prospect which has been your physical and psychological goal for more than two weeks now and looking over it from the Col de Jaman is a marvellous feeling. You could, alternatively, have enjoyed the Alps so much that the prospect of ending your odyssey appears mundane and anti-climactic. Never mind, it is not over yet.

Go out of the car park and turn left, following the yellow sign pointing to Montreux. Do not go via Les Avants, an alternative route to Montreux offered by the sign. A short way along the side of the mountain, below the car park, take a path forking to the right and signposted to Caux, a suburb of Montreux.

The path does not drop for some while but runs level along the side of the Dent du Jable. You can see why it is called 'Dent' when you look up at its tooth-shape. As you work your way round the peak you will see, when you look up, a great many huge metal barriers over a wide area of the mountainside, making it look like a vast terrace at a football ground. These are to guard against the danger of avalanches which have occurred due to the crumbly limestone which has sometimes broken off the peaks. Avalanches caused terrible disasters in 1714 and 1749, wiping out all human habitations which stood in their way and killing hundreds of people.

Your path follows the contours until Le Paccot and then slopes steeply down to join the railway. Cross on to the south side of this and after about half a kilometre cross back again. You are now just above Caux and this point signals the real end of the Alpine walk. It is now mostly a matter of finding your way through Caux and Glion, following the road for part of the way and cutting through woodland to avoid the tight zig-zags of the road up from Montreux. Follow the signs for Montreux through the centre of Glion and as you follow the road down on the edge of the suburb, look out for a sign saying 'Montreux direct'. This is indeed the direct way of getting to Montreux, but it is by no means an easy ride, for it consists of many hundreds of steps which you take down, down and down until you think there is no end to them. The rumble for the city gets ever nearer and you get tantalising glimpses of it through the trees, but you never seem to get there.

Finally you reach the bottom of the steps and it takes another ten minutes to thread your way through the streets of slick, cosmopolitan Montreux. If you want to perform the poetic, and in my opinion appropriate, act of touching the Waters of Leman as a gesture of completion, you would do well to make your way to the famous Casino right on the lake. In the gardens around this, you will find the odd place to dip your boots — or your whole self — in the lake and then lie back and exalt in your magnificent achievement.

Montreux is a fitting end to the Alpine Pass Route. Its much lower altitude is consistent with your final descent from the mountains; it is fast, flashy, expensive but beautiful and so seems the perfect place for a re-entry into civilisation. And it is by a lake, suggesting that, short of divine intervention, you simply could not walk any further in the same direction even if you wanted to.

Despite its wealth, it also caters for the less-rich in providing two campsites on the outskirts of the city at Villeneuve. If you are there during the period of the famous annual Jazz Festival, there may also be a free campsite available, evidently provided to dissuade the itinerant population, which comes flocking each summer, from dossing on the lawns and gardens around the Casino.

The Jazz Festival has a great international reputation and attracts some of the biggest names not only in jazz but also in blues, rock and their various permutations. This leavening of established jazz with more popular types of music does much to explain the considerable presence of the hippy fraternity and lends a rock — rather than jazz — festival air to the place.

It is worth spending a couple of days here to wind down and look around. The most famous tourist attraction is the Chateau de Chillon, the fairytale castle jutting out into the lake. Here you can mingle with the guided tours — or join one yourself and wander round a great many rooms dating from the ninth and tenth centuries; or you can descend to the dungeons where Francois Bonivard provided the inspiration for Byron's 'The Prisoner of Chillon'; or you can peer out of a window to see if there are any honey-haired damsels to be rescued from beneath the conical roofs of the chateau.

Running right past the Chateau but some way above it is the extraordinary viaduct which carries traffic above some of the lakeside towns to the south of Montreux right into the city centre. It is a marvel of engineering as it clings on to the side of the mountain.

Camping: There are two campsites on the outskirts of the city at Villeneuve. These can be easily reached on one of the city's fast and frequent buses.

Accommodation: Montreux's cheaper hotels include: The Riant-Chateau, 1820 Territet, Tel. 61 42 08; the Villa Germaine, 3 Av. Collonge, 1820 Territet, Tel. 61 27 44; the Beaux-Cedres, 34 Rue de la Gare, Tel. 61 52 13; and the Heidi, 3/9 Rue du Marche, Tel. 61 29 85. There is also a Youth Hostel in Montreux.

Postscript

After 206 miles and an ascent of many thousands of feet, what have you achieved? Suntans, hopefully, and hardened feet, certainly, but also the experience of a very beautiful country which can only be gained this way.

On the final approach to many a pass, it was sometimes difficult to see a reason why you subjected yourself to all that effort. But you only had to wait for the top when another wonderful view justified it all. Perhaps Sir Arnold Lunn in 'Mountains of Memory', put his finger on it when he wrote:

'How frequently the reward of beauty is associated with the dignity of toil, as if nature consciously reserves her noblest effects for those who take the trouble to earn them.'